Quinta—Essentia

A study of The Five Elements
of
Ether, Air, Fire, Water & Earth

Published in Great Britain 2003 by

MASTERWORKS INTERNATIONAL
27 Old Gloucester Street
London
WC1N 3XX
England

Tel: 0780 3173272
Email: books@masterworksinternational.com
Web: http://www.masterworksinternational.com

Copyright © 2003, Morag Campbell

ISBN: 0-9544450-0-7

Printed in the UK by Lightning Source

QUINTA ESSENTIA - THE FIVE ELEMENTS

By Morag Campbell

Contents

ACKNOWLEDGEMENTS

In the writing of this book I am indebted to the work of Dr Randolph Stone, founder of Polarity Therapy, and to Phil Young, who was my first Polarity teacher and whose in depth insights into the work have continued to spur me on in my own practice and understanding of this great body of work. The emphasis of the five elements in the healing art of Polarity has continued to be expanded over the years and have come to form a major part of my own practice and teaching of this truly holistic art. The elements offer a clear, precise way of understanding and interacting with the various manifestations of the life energy in the human body and mind, and represent a very naturalistic view point on life.

I would like to acknowledge the elemental communication work of Dr John Beaulieu PhD and Ruth Ann Pippenger and the influence they have had in my exploration of this aspect of the elements. My thanks also go to Bhagwant Singh Khalsa for his astute proof reading and enthusiasm for this project. I also wish to acknowledge the part played in the production of this book by a host of students and clients who pressed me into putting my ideas about the elements into one, easy to understand volume. Finally, I should like to acknowledge all my elemental friends in the natural world who exasperated, teased, comforted and inspired me as I went about the writing of this book, and who, even now, are most likely dancing across this open page as you read. Take care how you turn the pages!

IN YOUR ELEMENT

Long ago when the world was new and before man had begun to worship at the altar of the great god of science the ancients had a much more simple world view. Everything that they experienced could only be referenced to themselves and they came to know and explore the world through their five senses. To them all the known universe could either be seen, heard, tasted, smelled or touched. As their minds sought to make sense of the world that they found themselves in they came to realise that all that they knew fell into four main constituents. These constituents came to be known as the building blocks of all life, or the elements of air, fire, water and earth. They saw the great fireball in the sky and saw that it provided light. They felt its heat upon them and upon the land and experienced the cool darkness of night when the sun disappeared at the end of each day. Sensing the movement of the air all around them, breathing it in they felt it filling them and then its release back to the universe. They felt the breeze on their skin and the pressure in the atmosphere before a storm. They trusted the solid earth beneath their feet supporting them and all plant and animal life. They received the rain from the sky. Many early creation myths tell of how a mass of fire flew off from the sun forming solid matter, which became earth and as the steamy atmosphere that was created cooled, it separated into the gases of the air and the waters of the oceans and seas. These elements of air, fire, water and earth were present everywhere and in everything including man himself. However, in places it seemed that one element would hold sway over the others at any one time. Although all of the elements were present on the planet, when early man thought of the ground that he walked on it seemed to possess more of the element of earth than of the others even though it would have air and water within it and indeed even fire at its heart. As they came to know and then sought to understand the elements of nature they came to realise that there were fundamental forces that were beyond the domain of human control. They had an order and a "mind" of their own. To make sense of this mystery they found it reasonable to personify these elemental forces. Recognising their superior power to man they elevated and deified them so that the earth, the waters of the earth, the sky or air and the fiery places of the earth such as volcanoes were, they believed, inhabited by gods or spirits.

These gods, they believed, had all the archetypal qualities of man himself and yet were superhuman also. They ascribed human values and emotions to them so that when the rain fell gently on their crops, the rivers were full and ran with an abundance of fish, the sun smiled warmly on them then the gods were in a good mood and they were blessed. However if man were to upset them by his actions, these deities were, they believed, capable of unleashing the most formidable forces such as flood, earthquake, hurricane or fiery volcanic upheavals. They were, it seemed, totally amoral and no respecters of man nor beast; the torrential rain fell upon all, good or bad, young or old. Therefore, these gods of nature were to be revered, prayed to, sacrificed to and blessings asked from them for the benefit of

8

mankind. Man and gods lived side by side. Man respected the power of the gods and whenever possible lived in harmony with them.

Today in our modern technological society the gods of nature have been cast aside and man himself elevated to a much more exalted position in the scheme of things. These days we are above such beliefs it seems, choosing to believe rather in the sciences of meteorology, vulcanology or seismography to explain natural phenomena rather than ascribing them to the whim of some cantankerous spirit. These modern gods with their unpronounceable names have ousted out the old and more personal and readily accessible ones. With the old nature gods everyone could have an intimate and special relationship with them. They felt connected to them in a very real and tangible way. They asked questions of the gods and prayed to them directly and sure enough the gods would answer. The rain would fall or the earth yield up her bounty. Now the gods are so far removed from modern man that the deep and sacred connection to all things is lost to most of the modern population. However, all is not completely gone and somewhere deep in the psyche of all of us the memories of these old gods live on.

To the child the more simplistic way of looking at life is still the most natural. They, of all beings, remain faithful to the old gods. Yet even this innocent following is soon discouraged by an adult world that has been brainwashed into believing that every known phenomena has to be "proven" by scientific method. Trial by science is the new tool of the Inquisition. In true Celtic tradition, in the stories of my youth, for instance, every plant or tree, every stone or mountain was inhabited by tiny beings. These beings were of course invisible to all but children and those that had the gift of "sight." Today the elementals of the air live on as fairies. These flighty enchanting creatures care for all growing things. Ethereal and light as a feather they symbolise perfectly the freedom and changeability of the element of air. Fairies were rumoured to steal young babies from their cots, replacing the human child with a fairy child of their own which was named a "changeling." Even now young children still place their milk teeth under their pillows at night so that the tooth fairies may come to take the tooth and exchange it for money. This seeming magical ability to change one thing into another reflects the basic changeability that is the nature of air itself. You have to sit very quietly to catch a glimpse of these quick spirits, shy and elusive, as they tirelessly tend the flowers and trees.

The elemental associated with fire on the other hand is the salamander, but in the books of the nursery this element was often represented by the imp, a name that many a young child finds himself the recipient of even today. These cheeky, mischievous characters reflected the vitality and charismatic aspect of fire. Bright and cheerful they easily get out of control and into trouble. Just think of Shakespeare's character Puck in "A Mid-Summer Night's Dream" who leaps in the cup that the good wife is about to drink and bobs against her lip causing her to spill the brew or pulls away the stool from under the milk maid just as she is about to sit, causing her to fall, and you get some idea of the cheeky nature of the imp. Who knows how many innocent children, when asked who has broken a cup or written on the walls, are unjustly accused. Maybe we should listen more when they insist "it wasn't me!"

The element of earth lives on in the guise of a variety of similar characters known as elves, brownies or gnomes. These little people reflect the hard working qualities of this element, frequently working underground knowing how to successfully mine and utilise the earth's rich resources. For this reason they are often associated with money and wealth. In our everyday world these elementals have their colourful counterparts standing sentinel in many a garden the length and breadth of the British Isles. Stoic and silent they faithfully watch over their domain reminding us that hard work and diligence reaps the best rewards and the pot of gold at the end of the rainbow.

The Sprites or nymphs, mythological semi-divine maidens, reflect the element of water. Sensuous and seductive they were often accused of leading men to their deaths and many sailors were justly wary of these creatures that appeared often in the guise of beautiful women and mermaids. They were thought to distract the lonely seafarers and lead them astray onto nearby rocks where they were sucked down into the watery depths, never to be seen again. They epitomised the feminine quality of seduction and the power of magnetism.

So it seems, despite many efforts to the contrary, we have not totally given up on our early beliefs in these little elemental beings. We frequently encourage them into our lives to watch over our homes and our gardens and pay homage to the gods of nature which deep in our hearts we know are also a part of us. Projected outward and personified they still teach us that in order to live a healthy and harmonious life we must not upset any of the natural elements and forces within us that go to make us the human beings that we are.

The remnants of these elemental ways of thinking are also with us today in many figures of speech. We all know "air heads" and "fire balls" and talk of people as "flighty," "wet," or as being "all fired up" or "grounded." Despite all the scientific evidence around us the four elements are still as much a part of our lives today as they have always been. For the universe to function efficiently all the elements have to be balanced one with another in total harmony. All the elements are present in everything at all times. The proportions may change so that one or two seem to be very obvious at any one time but they are all there. Every element seeks to express itself. No one element is more important than another. They must all exist in harmony and in the appropriate proportions to ensure the balance of the universe. Over encourage one to the detriment of another and we upset the divine order that is behind the interplay of these fundamental building blocks of life. Together they make up the matrix in which all things exist and the fabric of our minds and bodies, our thoughts and feelings. They are the media through which we interface with each other and with life itself. Think what a mess we would all be in if there was not enough of the air element to support life, or too much of the fire element or insufficient earth. In fact we do not have to think very hard. As we look around us at the world in which we live we are already experiencing the reality of what it is like to have poor air quality with insufficient oxygen in it and the effects of global warming. The elements are already out of balance and there is disharmony. We are not taking notice of the elemental gods and they are angry! If we continue to take no notice and do not appease them by redressing the balance then they will wreak their revenge and it will be us who will perish.

In reality it is impossible to separate the elements from each other as they are so interdependent, but the human mind does have a need to categorise and to break things down into their component parts in order to understand their workings. In order that you may gain greater understanding of the workings of the elements in our lives this book seeks to explore each of the elements in their various manifestations in the life of man. It looks at their relationship to the personality through our astrological make-up and their manifestation in the different parts of the body and mind. We will see how the element that we are in at any one moment will affect our thinking processes, our interaction with those around us and what it means to be stuck in an element. We can come to recognise each element as it seeks expression through the voice and learn to modulate and flow with each of them for easier and clearer communication. The elements are also present in the food we eat and we can come to know why we prefer certain foods at certain times and why our diet can be so individual. Finally we will take a look at arguably the most illusive of all the elements and often the most ignored, the element of Ether, the fifth element.

You will come to recognise yourself in these pages and then to get to know yourself better. You will learn which of the elements are your friends, the ones you are happy and comfortable with, and which ones you are wary of, shying away from them because they seem unfamiliar or alien. To live life to the full it is important to recognise the manifestation of all the elements in our lives and come to count them all as our friends. They enrich our lives, giving it variety and depth. Not only will you be more in your own element, you will learn to be fully conversant in all the others as well!

SPIRIT OF AIR

When we think of air the quality of that element that springs to mind immediately is that of lightness and ease of movement. Despite the fact that the air around us is exerting a pressure of 14 pounds per square inch onto our bodies all the time, this does not fall into the realm of our everyday awareness and is something that the ancients would not have even considered. When they turned their faces to the wind what they registered was movement and a lightness that bordered on the intangible. What was this thing that surrounded them at all times, sometimes moving in gentle breezes that caressed their skin, cooling them on hot days, and sometimes raging with such a force that they had to battle to stand against it ? There is an all pervasiveness about air. It is a very communal element. Surrounding the earth, as it does, it envelopes all irrespective of who they are or where they might be. Invisible and intangible it is really only perceptible when it moves, which it does with an ease and a freedom not afforded to the other elements, being the least dense of them all. It is also noticeable by its absence of movement and we talk of still, calm days as airless. This ease of movement leads to the other main quality of this element, which is its changeability. A sudden gust can appear from nowhere or a high wind drop to nothing inexplicably in a moment. On a gusty day it refreshes and enlivens, as any teacher of young children will tell you, seeming to have the ability to excite and whip up their energy to a frenzy. On days when there is little movement of air we feel listless and heavy. It has the ability to fill up and lighten, sending our spirits soaring to engender a sense of freedom.

In nature the air is a wonderful medium for carrying things. Seeds, pollen, smoke, insects and birds are all transported through air, carried on the wind, sometimes half way round the globe. Wind is also used as a means of transport for humans . Caught in the billowing sails of ships it gives man a way of travelling great distances by harnessing the power of the wind to carry him over the oceans. Harnessed by land sails on the top of windmills it provides a means of grinding corn or bringing up water from the depths of the earth. Reading the wind is an art that many seafaring people in particular still practice. The direction of the wind, the temperature of it, the feel of it all convey information not only about the nature of the wind itself but also about the changing weather patterns. Many peoples still feel the air and look to the cloud formations or the patterns the wind makes on the water to divine valuable information about the coming weather or the availability of fish shoals.

Air is also the carrier of another important commodity: sound. It is this particular quality of air that ties the air element into communication. Whether it be the beating of drums, the rumble of thunder or the cry of a child, all sounds are carried on the air and communicate information. The Greeks had a word for it - Pneuma, which they related to divinely imparted knowledge or teaching. Inspiration, as we would now call this, can describe the physical act of drawing air into the lungs or equally apply to those thought processes that seem to come from outside oneself and are frequently ascribed to God.

The four elements have their counterparts in the four directions and Air is connected to the East. It is said to represent the energy of manifestation, things coming into being. The dawning of each day, as the sun rises, promises new beginnings. New life is established with the drawing of the first breath as the new born child establishes independent existence and a connection to his surroundings.

It is also interesting to note that our planet of Earth is surrounded by the air element. It helps to provide a protective atmosphere that envelops the planet, supports the life found there and provides the impetus that keeps it turning in space and powering the currents that swirl around it providing the changes in our weather. Without air there is no movement. Without movement there is no life !

THE AIR ELEMENT IN THE PERSONALITY

"I THINK - THEREFORE I AM"

When looking at how this element manifests in the personality, as with all the other elements, it is important to remember that the makeup of each person is a unique combination of all of the elements and very few people exhibit the qualities of just one element at all times but there are certain definable characteristics which are interesting to look at. When deciding if you have a lot of air in your make-up it can be useful to look at your astrological make-up. It is not my intention to go into great detail about the nature of astrology here. If you are interested there are many excellent books on the subject and an astrologer will be able to draw a chart for you which will show your elemental make-up clearly. When we talk of what astrological sign a person belongs to, what we are really referring to is their sun sign. Each astrological sign is governed by one of the four elements of air, fire, water and earth. Those signs which are governed by the air element are Gemini, Aquarius and Libra. As I said before however, whilst you may be one of the aforementioned air signs, the rest of your chart may have a predominance of planets in other signs which may be of other elements so it is important to keep the whole picture in view. For instance, many people present the energy of their rising sign to the world and this may be the element that you utilise the most in interaction with others.

Someone who utilises a lot of air energy will have their egoic sense of self firmly seated in their thinking capacities. Their greatest identification will be with their thinking abilities and as so much of our ego identification resides in our pride, they will be justly proud of these capabilities. They are great seekers of knowledge and information and always alert to new possibilities as they thrive on change. Having a lot of air energy in their make up can make them very inspirational, with quick minds which are inventive and alert. Eager to experience as much of life as possible, they may have a propensity to rush from one person or project to the next and this can lead to claims of indecisiveness or fickleness. Air people are naturally gregarious and very co-operative. They can

18

be great blenders of people, recognising talent in others so that they can organise and blend individuals into well co-ordinated groups. This means they can throw great parties ! They are usually great talkers and have a real need to communicate what they know, which can make them sound pompous! There is often an electric quality to these signs which can spill over into hyperactivity at times. They literally get pumped up, sometimes bouncing up and down and waving their arms around as they speak. Difficult to pin down, their natures can be described as flighty, but their lightness of being can literally bring a breath of fresh air to stagnant or boring situations. Quick to laugh they can be refreshing to be around, blowing away the cobwebs and lightening the situation. Manifesting more negatively they can be silly and flippant and come across as superficial or cold and aloof.

THE AIR ELEMENT AND THE BODY

People influenced by a lot of air energy can be tall and very graceful. The air body is often long and lean. They have a lot of energy, which tends to have an upward momentum, and this can be the reason that they can find it so hard to sit still. Even when standing and talking they tend to move about a lot, waving their arms in the air to accompany their speech.

The energy centre that governs the air element is to be found in the centre of the chest. Looking at the configuration of the rib cage and shoulder girdle can tell us a lot about how this energy is utilised in the individual. If the shoulders are slumped down, the chest becomes depressed, stifling the beating heart and blocking its emotional expression. With the body in this position, it becomes more difficult for the air element to be expressed and the whole system becomes sluggish. It becomes an effort to think, breathe and even move. On the other hand, a chronically held, over inflation of the rib cage can represent an over abundance of this element. The chest is constantly pumped up and the rib cage expanded to its full capacity. This pumped up appearance gives the illusion of self importance – literally looking bigger than you really are or feel. It is like the tiny puffer fish that fills itself with air when it is threatened to frighten off would be attackers. It is a bluff. For the person whose chest is chronically held in this position, there is a real fear of letting go and this represents a lack of trust in the life process. It is as if in fully breathing out, when the chest would naturally fall, there is death, because the fear is that in letting go nothing will come in to replace it.

Any holding of the chest and breathing will tend to hold our shoulders immobile. Indeed any threatening or loud behaviour around us as young children can result in a "startle reflex" becoming stuck in our body. Remember how your body reacts to loud noise. We tend to "jump," take a sharp intake of breath, and the shoulders head up around our ears. If this response becomes habituated our breathing becomes shallow and the shoulders immobile. Our shoulder blades have been called the "wings of life." If they are stuck to the rib cage then how can we fly ! It is as if they hold us down instead and we become "heavy hearted." The arms can be thought of as extensions of the heart for as the embryo grows in the womb the tiny arm buds seem to grow out of the organ itself and so the sense that is associated with the air element and the heart is the sense of touch. It is often through touch that we can express our true heartfelt feelings. If we close down on our heart centre we lose the ability to reach out and make contact with the world around us. We do not hug, or caress. We do not touch and therefore are untouched by life. We become cut off from it.

It is easy to see then that the air element manifests most strongly in our chests as breathing. The best way to ensure an adequate supply of the air element into the body is to make sure that we breathe well. Breathing is more than the drawing in and the letting go of air. It represents our ability to connect with Life itself. By the very act of breathing we open ourselves to Life and close again in the giving and receiving of this essential commodity. When our breathing is disturbed then we are disturbed. A disorder of the breath means disorder in ourselves, inhibiting our essential self and limiting us to the greater possibilities of life. Many people do not allow deep diaphragmatic breathing to take place. They breathe high up in the chest and the breath is weak and shallow which can lead to feelings of anxiety or panic. This kind of breathing is driven by the ego and closes us to the deeper expression of our essential self and our feelings. We do not connect with our bellies wherein lie our deeper emotions and more unconscious feelings. When breathing is deep and even then the whole body feels enlivened. Notice how you breathe when you are feeling depressed and you will see what I mean. A brisk walk or a game of tennis can be just the thing to shift your mood by getting that air element moving again as you increase your breathing capacity. It is essential that we relax and let go of the breath. Doing this completely will enable the air to automatically flood back into the lungs and there will be a natural ebb and flow to the procedure. Any holding here, as described above, which is evident in the chronically held concave, depressed chest as well as the chest that looks continually inflated , represents our inability to let go and trust to life. If we can soften the chest wall and allow the free passage of air in and out of the lungs we free ourselves of our inhibitions and hypertension and open ourselves to the freer expression of our essential being.

The heart also is linked strongly to the air element, situated as it is in the centre of the chest. We are quite rightly very protective of this vital organ both at a physical and emotional level. We tend to guard it well, not giving it away lightly or wearing it on our sleeves where it is vulnerable and can be easily damaged. Over zealous protecting of the heart can lead to excessive holding and tension in the chest. Holding back in this area creates a sunken chest and rounded upper back. We literally lock the heart away in the cage of the ribs, so much so that often we ourselves are not aware of it, until unable to be contained any longer and seeking expression, it rises up demanding our attention and threatening our very existence with an "attack" of heart. Conversely, someone who is said to be open hearted will have a body that reflects this attitude and the chest will be open and more exposed to the world. This is not to say that they will suffer no problems with this organ as a consequence. Some of the most open hearted people I know who can speak and act from the heart, express their heart felt feelings freely and are generous with their love have heart conditions. It is as if they are almost too open so that this area of the body becomes over exposed and therefore open to attack not from within but from without. As a consequence they are often easily hurt and damaged by other people's words and actions.

The nervous system is another aspect of the body that is strongly influenced by this element. All pervasive, it transmits messages with lightening speed. It acts as a communication network both sending and receiving messages that keep us in touch with what is going on around us. A person with a lot of air energy usually has a lot of nervous energy and can suffer as a consequence. Conditions of the nervous system such as Parkinsons, Multiple Sclerosis or Motor Neurone Disease are a problem with this element. Too much air energy in the system can produce an overactive nervous system leading to nervous exhaustion or panic attacks, or it can affect the digestive predominately where it manifests as flatulence and bloating. The production of gas in our body, caused by poor digestion or intolerance to certain foods, can cause havoc to our whole system. Not only does it cause considerable pain, discomfort and distension in the abdomen but can also lead to headaches, neck pain and pains in the limbs such as the calf muscles. The ease of movement of air seems to enable this particular problem to surface anywhere with disastrous results sending shooting pains all over our body.

Too little air on the other hand leads to conditions such as asthma, poor circulation and general muscle spasm. It can slow down the process of digestion and lead to stagnation in the gut causing constipation.

An imbalance in this element causes all the movement capabilities of our body to suffer accordingly. Because the air element is the impetus or impulse behind all movement it is easy to see that it governs all the movement capabilities in our body, the most obvious of these being the beating of the heart, the pulsing of blood through the arteries and veins, the rise and fall of the ribs in breathing and the passage of food through the body during the process of peristalsis. However this element also controls all the other movements of the body that are present all the time below our normal level of awareness such as all the pulsations of the various organs, the impulses of our nervous systems and even the minute vibrations of every single cell in our body. Even when we are doing nothing we are far from still; in fact, in reality our bodies are constantly vibrating and pulsating. At a more gross physical level, all our movement capabilities such as walking, running and all physical activities have to do with the influence of the air element.

In astrology, the sign of Gemini is said to have influence over the shoulders and arms as well as the lungs and respiration and we have seen how an imbalance in the air energy in the body particularly affects these parts. Libra's rule over the kidneys can lead to hormonal problems in times of stress as more and more adrenalin is pumped out around the body the more anxious and hyperactive we become. Air imbalances can therefore affect these organs as well as lead to pain and tension, with the associated immobility, in the region of the lower back. High blood pressure is also thought of as a problem with this element because of its connection to the heart and circulation as well as the effects of the

24

kidneys on this condition. Low blood pressure could be seen as a lack of air energy in the system whereas high blood pressure would seem to indicate a build up of this element. Problems with the air element can also manifest in the lower legs as cramps or varicose veins and pain and immobility around the ankles. Those born under the air sign of Aquarius could also fall prey to airy conditions. Sometimes a disturbance in the air element manifests in a variety of non-specific conditions that can mysteriously disappear as easily as they came, leading to some frustration on the part of patient and doctor alike!

THE AIR ELEMENT AND THE MIND

It could be said that Air is the element of mind as it governs our thought processes. Thoughts are nebulous things. Amazingly fast moving, we can think much faster than we can speak. Thoughts can be hard to get hold of leading to an ability to change our minds in the wink of an eye. As I said before, the airy mind is particularly quick and alert and air people are great thinkers. The airy mind thrives on abundant activity. Like baby fledglings, with constantly demanding beaks open wide, air people need new ideas and innovations to constantly feed their all consuming minds. If this is taken to excess they can become extremely boastful of their acquired knowledge and strut around like cocky bantams with their chests puffed up before them. They can seek knowledge for the sake of knowledge and it often needs to be blended and tempered with the wisdom of experience. The continuous need for input means that if there is not sufficient information externally to stimulate, they will manufacture their own and a fertile imagination is born.

Like a child constantly asking "why" they seek to broaden their understanding of the relationships between people and concepts. In doing so they often make intellectual leaps and connections that can so often lead to brilliant new and innovative ideas. Air knows no boundaries, it just flows around and through seeking the easiest passage. This can also be a metaphor for the air person's attitude to life. When the going gets tough, the air person may well get going, moving swiftly and easily on to pastures new. Just as air knows no boundaries, the mind itself, which is ruled by this element, has no limitations only those imposed upon it by itself. This lack of boundaries and sense of detachment however, can if taken to extreme, lead to conditions such as schizophrenia, where the boundaries of self and other, real and imagined are blurred.

The air personality likes to move out into the world, discovering, experimenting, and constantly testing the boundaries of what is possible. They know what they want and they set out to get it. After all, the sky is the limit for air people. Taken to extreme, this constant wanting can manifest in competitiveness and they can turn to manipulation in order to gratify their desires. If this negative trait continues, they can become deceitful and insensitive. Like a small child in a sweet shop they don't see why they can't have everything that they want now! Over time, if their needs are not met (and they rarely are because there is a tendency to want more and more, and to move on to the next thing that takes their fancy without waiting to manifest their first wants), they begin to feel burdened by their want and crushed when they cannot achieve it. Patience is not an airy trait.

The rational, airy mind ever seeking understanding that can lead to a great intellectual evaluation of life can lead to the criticism that air types live in their heads. They can remain emotionally detached from circumstances, which of course has good and bad connotations. In a heated argument it can have definite advantages and can even make outwitting your antagonist or joking your way out of a tricky situation a distinct possibility. However, in a more intimate relationship this air of detachment can be problematic leading to charges of inability to commit for instance. It can be cold logic for the airy type, unlike the impassioned emotional responses of the water element. The airy mind can impress and uplift others, stunning them with the speed and variety of its thought processes. People with a lot of this element can manifest a quick wit and a quirky sense of humour that makes them refreshingly fun to be around. However, this comes across to some people as frivolous behaviour especially if you are the one in a serious mood.

Air types can be so pre-occupied with thinking that they never actually get anything done. Flitting from one good idea to the next like a frenzied butterfly, their challenge is to harness these brilliant thoughts before they escape and make them manifest, bringing them to fruition, otherwise they are justifiably accused of being just full of hot air!

THE AIR ELEMENT IN COMMUNICATION

Communication is a learned process. As we look at how the various elements manifest themselves through this process we will recognise that there are positive and more negative expressions of these energies. Being a learned process it is possible to learn new means of communication that are more effective in any given circumstance. If you recognise that you have a tendency to a more negative mode of communication, then train yourself to turn it around. You will find it is worth the effort and the practice. Good clear communication is worth its weight in gold and you will find your life enriched and be justly rewarded for your efforts.

The air element can be said to be the element of communication as air people love to talk. Thoughts and conversation are synonymous. You cannot have one without the other although this is challenged by some individuals, leading to the popular saying "please engage brain before opening mouth." Indeed, all of our internal communication is just us talking to ourselves. When we decide to engage another person or persons we are said to be communicating with them and part of that communication is to inform them of our internal thoughts. As we speak we make various sounds by the passage of air from the lungs over the vocal chords and these sounds are then carried on the air to be received by another individual. Airy people love to talk and when they do, there is often a distinct quality to the voice that is easily identifiable as air. There is a clearly audible, breathy quality to it. Good examples are Marilyn Monroe or the archetypal hippie. In these examples the speech is quite slow and the breath noticeably present but some air people can get so carried away with ideas, that they come thick and fast and their constantly changing minds make their speech extremely rapid, so much so that they constantly gasp for breath and their voice can get higher and higher! In this instance, they bounce from one idea to the next, often changing topic in the process, so that it can be extremely difficult to follow their line of thought. The classic "butterfly mind!" This can lead to extreme confusion on the part of both speaker and listener. It can be hard to keep them on track in a conversation. Their minds are so quick that they have thought of every eventuality and permutation, dismissed the unworkable ones, deviated and side tracked into related areas and come back to the original point before you have registered more than the first sentence or two and they have the need to verbalise every thought process as it is occurring.

Air types can be extremely hard to pin down - try getting hold of a handful of air ! Sometimes, just when you think you have grasped the situation they come up with yet another brilliant idea to inspire you. Air people seem to use their hands as a major aid to communication and you can get the feeling that if you tied their hands behind their backs you would render them mute. All this airiness can leave you feeling worn out as you battle to keep up with them. However, they can be inspiring speakers and good debaters with a keen wit. Their ability to maintain a certain detachment from the situation means that they can "rise above" the situation to get a different perspective on it which can be very refreshing and innovative.

Air people can however be great procrastinators. There is always some new idea or some new venture that is far more important than the job in hand and they frequently have more than one project on the go at once, all in various stages of completion. Remember their challenge is to manifest some of these great ideas that they have and bring them to fruition.

Possessing a great sense of freedom and a pathological fear of being tied down can make air types masters of the technique of evasion which means that they can be very manipulative, deliberately engendering an air of confusion. Evasion is a technique that an air person can use to their advantage. Sometimes they side track the issue by changing topic overtly as in the following snippet of conversation:

"Did you pick up the laundry for me this morning as I asked you to?"

An airy reply might be

"Well it was so hot today. Gosh, I've just realised I haven't had a drink since lunchtime. I'm so incredibly thirsty. Are you thirsty? Can I get you a drink?"

Sometimes it is done so subtly, as in the next example, that you think that you have been heard and answered but somehow the reply has just slid by you and nine times out of ten you didn't even notice.

"I am fed up having to make all the phone calls in this house. I am not going to do it any more. Do you hear?"

Air response:

"Yes. I hear you. That's perfectly clear. You are not going to make any more calls."

The assumption on the part of the first speaker is that they have been heard and understood and that if they are not going to make any more calls then the other person has to make them. However, this is not what the second person has actually said. It is only later when the first speaker wonders why no calls have been made that he realises that he was not answered directly at all. This is very poor communication. The first speaker made the error of assuming that a certain action would be forthcoming and it is obviously impossible to have effective communication with someone who is constantly evading the issue or declining to take responsibility. A person using an airy method of communication will never respond directly to your questioning and may frequently try to distract you, as witnessed in the first example above, by changing topic. Remember how hard it can be to pin air people down, and if both of you are communicating in this negative way then real harm can be done to both parties. If you ask a question and receive an evasive response then it seems to you that you are not really being heard and therefore the message comes across as you don't really matter. It is as if the other person is cancelling you out. You cannot be very important if you do not even warrant an answer to your concerns.

Imagine what it is like to feel that you are never really heard or effectively answered . If both parties in the communication process are using this mode of communication then they are effectively avoiding one another. In this kind of communication neither party feels valued and the communication process is totally ineffective. This kind of interaction is potentially one of the most damaging ones that we can indulge in with neither party feeling heard or answered because they are effectively cancelling each other out. They are, to quote Shakespeare, "full of sound, signifying nothing." Imagine what it must be like to be in a family where for instance both parents are using this kind of communication. Pretty soon our self esteem and our sense of self is eroded away and we can begin to feel that we do not really exist. We may even begin to doubt our sanity. The feelings that underlie this kind of communication are "no one cares what I say anyway" and "I don't want to be here."

Direct questioning makes air people feel put on the spot. Being airy they are particularly susceptible to pressure and will do anything to wriggle out from under. By not responding appropriately and avoiding eye contact it is as if they are trying to appear invisible, conveying that they do not wish to be engaged. When communicating with someone of this sort, keep bringing them back to the topic, be patient, wait until they feel able to answer and get them to look you in the eye if possible. Remember that the evasion is done out of fear and you have to win their trust and let them know that you really value what they have to say.

Air used in a positive way in the communication process can mean the speaker can metaphorically step back from the discussion and use the power of detachment to disengage from the emotionality of the situation to get a clear overview of what is going on and add fresh insight. In an emotionally charged situation the air responses might go something like this:

"OK, I think we need to take a break right now and get some fresh air. Let's meet back in 30 minutes. I have

been listening to both sides of this argument and I think I have an idea for moving this project forward that will satisfy you both."

When to use your air element communication is an important question. You will need to introduce more air into a situation if things are becoming very emotionally charged or if the conversation is getting bogged down and going nowhere. Remember that air can be used as a way of distracting and this can have positive as well as negative effects. Mothers use this type of communication a lot to distract a crying child to get their attention focused on something else. Use it to inspire others.

THE AIR ELEMENT AND DIET

Food and the elements can be classified in two ways. One of the simplest ways of thinking about foods that possess an abundance of the air element is to think of the foods that grow surrounded by this particular element, that is the foods that grow high up above the surface of the earth in the trees. These include the fruits and nuts such as lemons, limes, grapefruit, tangerines, oranges, pineapples, almonds, pecans and cashew nuts. Remember that the major quality of air is movement and these foods are the ones we turn to encourage our digestive systems to work more speedily. The other way of classifying an element is by taste and the taste that defines the air element is sourness. The most obvious example of a pure air food is lemon but other examples would be rhubarb and tomatoes. A sour tasting fruit is a good way of introducing the air element into our bodies. A useful analogy of our digestive process is a furnace. At its centre is a fiery oven that breaks the food down. This fire has to be fed with the correct amount of fuel, i.e., food and the correct proportion of air for effective combustion. The right combination of the air and fire element in the body is vital for good digestion. People who have a problem with the air element, like those with a tendency to asthma, can find that eating a meal makes breathing more difficult as all the air energy in their bodies is being used in the process of digestion. A couple of teaspoons of lemon juice prior to eating gives an immediate top up to the air element and can ensure that there is sufficient for both functions in the body. The sour tasting yoghurts and fermented cheeses like Stilton, Camembert and Danish Blue also introduce this element to our systems. A craving for these types of foods can indicate a lack in this element as the body seeks to remedy the imbalance. However, if you have a lot of air in your makeup or you work at a sedentary job which demands brain power as opposed to physical strength then you will find yourself drawn to these foods which on the whole are light and easy to digest so they will not divert too much energy from elsewhere, such as the head, leaving you feeling muzzy and thick headed.

It is worth pointing out again here that what we are aiming for is balance. Just the right amount of air foods in our diet ensures that we have the correct proportion for healthy functioning of our digestive system. Too little, and the food is not digested easily and hangs around the digestive tract for too long, fermenting and causing stomach problems, indigestion and constipation. Clogging up our systems leads to a build up of toxicity producing headaches, skin problems, lethargy and bowel problems like colitis. Too much of the air foods in the diet or eating too many oxidising foods such as a fresh fruit salad where the fruit is cut up into small pieces thus increasing the surface area which oxidises rapidly when exposed to the air can give us problems too. They can cause poor breakdown of food, gas trouble and bloating which can give rise to considerable pain and discomfort. Gas travels around the body rather like an air lock in your central heating system and you know how inconvenient and noisy that can be!

THE AIR ELEMENT RELATIONSHIPS

When looking at how the elements combine in our system it is once again worth looking at how the elements interact in nature. The old adage "as within, so without" applies here. Looking at the interaction of the elements in nature goes a long way to helping us understand the interaction of the elements within us. It is also important to look at how any element combines with any other of the elements in three ways. One, what is the effect when the proportions are just right, producing a balanced interaction; two, what are the effects when one element is in excess; and three, what are the effects when in depletion.

When air is in a balanced combination with fire it sustains it allowing it to burn freely. One could say that air feeds fire. In nature fire needs oxygen in order to burn but in the correct proportion. Too little air and the fire is starved and glows weakly, finally going out altogether when all the oxygen is used up. Too much air has the effect of fanning the fire causing it to burn more fiercely, providing it has enough material to consume, and it consumes it at a rapid rate. Remember the speed at which great forest fires can spread. An excess of air, fueling the fire in the body can lead to an overactive digestion with food passing through the system too rapidly for good absorption, or causing an overproduction of hydrochloric acid and bile leading to stomach ulcers and gall stones. Too much air can also put the fire out completely and again digestion suffers. The effect on the mind is to make our thinking vacuous and unclear .

Balanced air has a refreshing and enlivening effect on the water element. Introducing the correct amount of air oxygenates the water allowing it to support life. With insufficient air the water can become stagnant and polluted. Think what happens to a fish tank if it is not oxygenated regularly. Think of the effects of that kind of stagnation in the body ! In this case for example, the lymphatic system struggles, producing oedema and an over abundance of mucus in the lungs. Too much air however can whip up the water causing rapid evaporation leading to a severe depletion of the water element in time which can manifest as stiffness in the joints, constipation and a general lack of flexibility in the body and mind. It literally dries them out. Something to bear in mind considering the human body is mostly water.

Air has a similar effect on the earth element in that it enlivens it and gives it a good texture that again can support animal and plant life. A rich loam soil has a crumbly texture and a sweet smell. Too little air and the earth can be waterlogged and sour, too much and it can dry out, turn to dust and blow away. As the earth energy rules the digestion and elimination to a great extent, these functions would be disrupted by a lack or surplus of air.

GETTING IN TOUCH WITH AIR

➢ Remember Air is the element of change. If you are feeling stuck, bogged down or in a rut you will need to get things moving again. Take a holiday to provide a change of scene and stimulus. If that is not possible then get an exciting fiction book from the library and stimulate your mind and imagination to break away from habitual thought patterns.

➢ Breathing exercises are of course an excellent way of introducing more of this element into your life. Take some exercise if you tend to lead a sedentary life or try the following aid to increasing your breathing.

➢ Stand with your feet shoulder width apart and with feet parallel as if on railway lines. Keep your knees bent and tuck your pelvis under as if about to sit down. Try to keep your shoulders down and relaxed whilst performing this exercise. Raise your arms in front of you to shoulder height and connect the thumb and fore finger of each hand as if taking two pinches of salt. Take a long slow breath in and as you do so draw the hands apart until they are stretched out to the sides of your body. Do not lock your elbows. Try to make the breath last for the whole of the movement so the speed of the movement will depend on how long it takes to draw in the breath. At the end of this movement keep the thumbs and fingers together but turn the hands palm up towards the ceiling. Breathing out draw the hands back together again in front of you until they meet. Be aware of your breath as you repeat this exercise as many times as feels comfortable. Does it move in and out of the lungs in a steady, smooth stream or do you find yourself running out of air and gasping for breath ? Does the chest feel restricted or the shoulders ache? Do not force either the breath or the movements. With steady practice you will find that the breath begins to flow more easily and in fact lasts for much longer than it used to and that the body eventually seems to move at the behest of the breath. If you have difficulty standing still for long periods and this slow meditative exercise seems boring— Persevere. If you are fidgety you have too much air in your system and this will help regulate it. If you have movement problems or are confined to a chair the exercise can be done very effectively from a seated position.

➢ Taking up some kind of movement form such as dance or Tai Chi can get this element going again. Look for a class in your area.

➢ Make a list of those areas of your life in which you feel stuck. Maybe you feel your job is going nowhere or there is a stagnation in your personal relationships. Think of ways to breathe new life into them. Use your imagination, become inspired.

➢ Go out on a windy day and feel the effect on your body and your emotions. Do you feel invigorated and enlivened? Maybe it has blown away the

38

cobwebs and had a cleansing effect on your aura, or maybe you feel buffeted and worn out by it and more than slightly agitated. Make a note of your findings as they will tell you something about how you deal with Air.

> The use of sound to clear the energy centres is a very practical and rewarding way of getting in touch with an energy and ensuring its balanced expression. Stand with your feet apart, knees relaxed, and keep your diaphragm and throat as relaxed as possible. Take a deep breath. As you let the breath out make the sound "AH." Make the sound last as long as you can so the breath will come out in a controlled way rather than in a short expulsion of air. Open the mouth as wide as possible in a vertical direction and relax the tongue to the floor of the mouth. You will have to relax the jaw joint. Feel how your body is resonating and vibrating to this particular sound. If you find it difficult, persevere, until the "AH" sound is long and rounded. Practice where you will not be disturbed. After a few minutes, stop and observe both yourself and the feeling in the room around you. It will help to begin the exercises with your arms held in a circle in front of you with fingertips touching, just as if you are hugging. Then as you sound, slowly expand the arms out to the side to open up and expose the chest.

SPIRIT OF FIRE

The fire element is easily recognisable by its main qualities of light and heat. The ancients were acutely aware of the great fire ball in the sky that came each day bringing light and warmth to the land, and sun worship was an important part of many early cultures. Even today many of us in Europe make an annual pilgrimage to the south of France, Italy or Spain to worship this deity (sadly it does not visit the British Isles that frequently so we have to go in search of it). In many religious traditions fire is seen as a symbol of the divine. The saints are depicted with light emanating from them and a celestial flame still burns at many altars across the world. Candles are lit at many religious ceremonies to represent the bringing of light as knowledge and spiritual fire into the world. During the long, dark days of winter, when it seems the sun has deserted the land, bonfires symbolically bring light and warmth back into the lives of men and encourage the sun's return. The winter solstice, when fires are traditionally ignited, welcomes the coming of the new sun as the days begin to lengthen again. In the Christian tradition this time of year is also celebrated as the birth of Christ—the celebration of the "son" appearing. Fire was thought to bring divine enlightenment and was often seen as being superior to the other elements. John the Baptist baptised with water but he spoke of one called Christ who was to come and who would baptise with Fire. The Sufi tradition speaks of fire as the Holy Spirit.

Early man brought fire into his home to warm it, to light its dark recesses and to cook his food. Prior to this his experience of fire, apart from the sun, was in the form of volcanic eruptions or spontaneous fires started by lightening bolts. When man learnt the secret of fire he found a way to harness this particular energy so that it served him well and today we have followed on from those early lessons. But we must never forget the power of fire and its volatile nature. It can flare up in a moment and get easily out of control making it hard to handle and leading to rapid wide spread destruction on occasions.

Fire has always held a fascination for man. The combination of light, heat and sound are fascinating to us and tap into our primal instincts for warmth and comfort. It is amazingly lively and charismatic. Try sitting in a room with a fire and not watching it. It demands attention and respect. Fire is often used as a form of protection and defence. Camp fires are lit to keep wild animals at bay, since all creatures instinctively have a healthy respect for this element, and fires set along the perimeter of an encampment act as a warning to all who come near. Its brightness cheers us and keeps the demons in the dark corners of our own minds in their place. One small night light in a room can make the difference between a restful night's sleep and a fitful, wakeful one where half an eye is kept open to watch for monsters. In today's world we only occasionally have the need to light protective fires, but fire power is still used as a defensive and offensive strategy. The explosive might of this element, recognised in earlier times, for instance, in the personification of Mars the god of war, has been harnessed by man into our many weapons. Ever since the production of gunpowder and then the first atomic bomb man has found a way to mimic the colossal might of fire that previously had only been assigned to the realm of the gods. Yet, mighty as today's modern weapons are, they pale into insignificance against the power of the natural element. The amount of fire power or fire arms that a person or a country possesses determines both their defensive and antagonistic capabilities. Like the ancient Greek gods on Mount Olympus who would rain lightening bolts on the hapless humans below, we humans believe ourselves elevated to this deified state, hurling our thunderbolts at one another and taking on the power of life and death.

There are of course other aspects to this element and fire can be extremely cleansing in nature. A bush fire as well as destroying vegetation also destroys many pests and diseases so that new growth is promoted which is stronger and healthier than the old. At another level we speak of being cleansed by spiritual fire so as to be born again. Having to undergo "trial by fire" in today's world means learning from hard experience from which we cannot help but be changed. This leads to another aspect of fire, which is the magical quality of transformation. Fire's ability to change the nature of substances has long been known and marvelled at. A variety of metals when heated to melting point in a furnace are transformed into a new amalgam with different properties. The blacksmith uses the power of fire to bend metal to his will in order to make horseshoes, and the master sword maker use fire to temper his blades. Even humble clay when "fired" is transformed into usable pottery. Because of man's natural fear of fire it is an element that we constantly pit ourselves against. Fire walking and fire eating are ways

42

of coming to terms with this element that some find useful.

Will power is another aspect of the fire element. It is interesting that so many of our modern addictions involve this element, such as smoking, alcohol, cocaine, etc. All require will power in order to overcome the craving that these substances create—a case of "fighting fire with fire" maybe.

THE FIRE ELEMENT IN THE PERSONALITY

" I CREATE—THEREFORE I AM "

Fire people identify with their creative abilities. Often they possess great visionary qualities and are masters of setting goals and structuring their lives to achieve them. To this end they are generally outward going, decisive and pioneering. They have warm, sunny dispositions and can very optimistic and jolly—the "hale fellow well met" type. They are often hard working and ambitious. However, they do like to be the boss and can have a hard time taking orders from others. Leos especially can make good rulers, or more negatively, great dictators. The fire energy is an outward, yang energy and fiery types would do well to learn self-reflection. They can become so full of their own brilliance and importance that they totally ignore any feedback from others or fail to realise the consequences of their actions. Taken to an extreme, the feelings of omnipotence can lead to megalomania and insanity. Those born under the fire signs of Aries, Leo or Sagittarius are often go-getters and risk takers. They are very goal oriented, know what they want—and go for it, often at the expense of all who get in their way. They can appear very opinionated and somewhat dogmatic. Unlike the air signs they can have a hard job changing their minds so they are not easily open to persuasion. This refusal to deviate from a chosen direction can lead to obsessive behaviour. To function purposefully their fire has to be linked to another of the elements to bring about balance.

In their great need to get where they are going the fire type can aggressively surge forward in the pursuit of some goal in a very direct manner, blazing a trail as they go, running rough shod over the ideas and feelings of others. They do have to guard against burning out all together in the aftermath of all this activity. Very often they do not know how to stop until it is too late when the people around them will let them know in no uncertain terms that they have overstepped the mark, or their bodies give out and they are forced to rest. Fiery people have a reputation for being quick tempered. They tend to blow their tops easily, exploding into rages at the drop of a hat, but then returning to a warm friendly glow immediately afterwards. Their driving ambitions can make them appear selfish and uncaring to some and their charismatic and unconventional personalities mean that they can easily impose their will on others and bully people into getting what they want. They can often be larger than life characters who can generate a great deal of enthusiasm and inspirational zeal and, unlike the airhead, they get the job done! As individuals they can be intensely passionate and full of desire. Their larger than life character can outshine many others but this same fire energy can also be utilised to enlighten. The fire energy gives clarity to thought. It can illuminate an idea and then express it clearly and directly. The fire person is decisive with a razor sharp intellect that can cut through the dross to get to the heart of the matter in moments. It is incisive and bold.

FIRE ELEMENT AND THE BODY

The fire body is of medium height and build and those individuals who are heavily influenced by this element are usually very strong and wiry. The energy centre for this element is to found in the solar plexus. Balanced fire gives a healthy glow to our skin, a sparkle to our eyes and a general sense of vitality and robust good health. If we have an excess of fire energy it can lead to a large belly and a more rotund appearance. As I said, one of the main qualities of fire is its heat producing capability. Therefore the region of the solar plexus and especially the liver, which is the largest heat producing organ in the body, come under the influence of the fire element. Our bodies work efficiently within a very small temperature range and it is important that this temperature is adhered to. A few degrees too high and we produce fever where the body literally burns up. Here is an example of the cleansing effect of fire in action. The high temperature produces an adverse environment for invading organisms and the excessive fire drives off the water in our body as sweat, which cleanses the body of toxins. So critical is our body temperature that the successful management of a fever can mean the difference between life and death especially in the days before modern drugs. It is equally critical to maintain the

45

core temperature of the body which can also be life threatening if it slips to dangerously low levels, leading to hypothermia and eventual death. The protective function of fire can be seen at play here also. A good maintenance of the fire element in the body ensures a high level of vitality, and when the vitality is high then the immune system functions efficiently maintaining good health. If our vitality drops for some reason, energy levels are lowered and that is when we succumb to disease. We need a good supply of fire to give us the power to fight infection and win!

The digestive region of the body is also associated with the fire element as it is concerned with the breakdown of food. The stomach produces fiery hydrochloric acid in just the right amount. Too little leads to incomplete breakdown of food which then lies in the stomach too long and can lead to incomplete absorption of nutrients further on in the system as well as symptoms of indigestion. Too much fire can manifest as stomach or duodenal ulcers as the gastric juices literally burn into the linings of these organs. The gall bladder also is thought of as a fiery organ. It secretes bile, a strongly alkaline fluid, which is never the less a highly caustic fiery substance. Feelings of bitterness, hatred or resentment can crystalise here in the form of gall stones.

Many of us have a problem dealing with fire in our lives and are somewhat afraid of it, and rightly so as fire has a habit of flaring up at a moment's notice quickly getting out of control. The fire energy is often expressed as anger. An inability to deal with this emotion causes us to hold excessive tension in the region of the solar plexus, causing considerable contraction here that in

46

some cases bows the body forward, pulling down the chest which effectively starves the fire of air by restricting breathing. If the fire is not being fed, the lack of air will effectively shut down the energy centre of this element. Immobilising the diaphragm ensures that we keep a tight lid on our emotional expression. The respiratory diaphragm can act rather like the lid on a pressure cooker. An enormous pressure of emotion can be held down in this way, with short bursts of expression escaping every so often as we need to let off steam. These short releases only serve to stop the whole system exploding and do not address the cause of the holding in the first place.

It is obvious the kind of physical problems that are created by this kind of body structuring. Stuck in this chronic flexor contraction we take on the appearance of a whipped dog. There is no way that the fire element is going to be able to express itself naturally within the body in this state. Each element seeks expression and one way or another it will be seen and heard. If it is not expressed externally in words and actions then it is expressed internally as a symptom. Result—stomach ulcers, liver problems and problems with the rest of the digestive tract as the organs are restricted. When the diaphragm is moving as in good breathing it constantly massages these organs and aids in the passage of food through the gut. The organs of the abdomen need sufficient space in which to function well; each has its own rhythm and natural vibratory level for optimum functioning and if all the organs are squashed in on each other then their functioning is impaired. All this trapped fire energy is added to an already fiery area and the organs there will suffer accordingly. The restriction in the chest due to the bowing effect set up by the tightening of the diaphragm can lead to problems like asthma—and all because the fire energy is not allowed to express itself naturally.

Another problem that can arise if the fire is not given natural expression is the production of rashes, spots and acne. We even use the expression "an angry rash" to describe such conditions and they frequently appear in areas of the body that are particularly associated with the fire element such as the head or the region of the solar plexus. The condition know as Shingles for instance often starts at the waist and can spread all around the body at this level whilst the other common site for it to occur is on the face.

The head is a prime site for the expression of fire energy. We talk of someone as being a "hot head" or "blowing her top." Certainly a lot of heat is lost from the body via the head, hence the need for wearing a hat in very cold weather. We can see the fire energy clearly when someone is hot or angry as their face gets redder and redder or when they blush with embarrassment. Too much alcohol or "fire water" produces the same flushed appearance, which can become permanent for those with a drink problem. Incidentally, many people who are unable to express the fire element naturally turn to alcohol as a way of stimulating this particular energy. They literally add fire to their systems and the most common results of drinking are to enable the person to freely express their joyfulness and become more outgoing or conversely to express their anger and aggression. These are all qualities of fire. Smoking is another way in which people can emulate this energy taking on the appearance of fiery, smoke breathing dragons.

The part of the head where the fire element can be most clearly seen is the eyes. They are the sense organs through which we perceive light. There is also an internal light that can be seen in the eyes, "Her eyes lit up when she saw the present." "Her eyes shone with delight." "His eyes burned into me," and "There was a twinkle in his eye as he spoke" are all common modes of speech to illustrate, or should I say, illuminate the point. Our general health and vitality can be read in our eyes. Well-balanced fire leads to a good complexion with bright, alert eyes. Too much fire can mean a ruddy complexion and staring, bulbous eyes. Too little gives a pale skin and dull, listless eyes that are lacking in energy and interest. A disturbance of fire energy in the head can lead to headaches. Often the fire imbalance affects the digestive system, too. Migraine headaches are a classic fire problem affecting the head, the digestive system and the eyes, with disturbed vision as a classic symptom. Conjunctivitis, where the eyes become red and irritated, is another fire problem.

The thighs are another area where fire energy is very perceivable. The fiery personality sets a goal and goes for it. They have a strong sense of direction but need good legs to take them there or they become stuck. That fire energy makes the legs strong and the step purposeful. If we are lacking in fire the legs become weak, ill defined, shaky and no longer support us. In addition to the belly, the thighs are another part of the body where there is a tendency to store this particular energy. This

49

seems to be more the case for women where so called "Jodhpur thighs" are common. It is often culturally frowned upon for women to express their fire energy openly. They should not be loud, vivacious, aggressive or angry. "Sugar and spice and all things nice—that's what little girls are made of !"

Fire is also the element of sexual passion. Again, there are many sayings that illustrate the connection between this element and desire. We can "have the hots" for someone, or "burn with desire." Former partners are commonly known as "old flames." Poorly functioning fire can lead to problems with impotency and low sex drive. Too much fire channelled into a sexual outlet and watch out! It is easy to be carried away in the heat of the moment!

The fire element can also be linked to the sympathetic branch of the autonomic nervous system. As we have heard fire people are great "doers," rarely sitting still for a minute. This constant need for achievement means that the sympathetic nervous system is "switched on" for long periods of time. Indeed, it may never actually get switched off, so the person stays sympathetic dominant and is classified as a Type A personality, i.e., someone who is prone to high levels of stress. One of the problems of being sympathetic dominant is that the endocrine system, and especially the adrenal glands, are switched on all the time pumping out adrenaline into the system which keeps the heart rate high and the body in a constant state of alertness. It is the primitive "fight or flight" response which sets us up to deal with dangerous situations. However, these days we are less likely to run into an encounter with a lion and more likely to have to get ourselves out of a tricky traffic situation. These adrenaline rushes give a high, intense feeling of "aliveness." Whilst the human body is designed for this on occasions, such as in times of danger, it does not cope well with this activity over a prolonged period. The go-getting pace of life lived by most fire people rarely allows for rest times and they find themselves in a constant state of alert day in, day out. Such states of high excitement can be extremely addictive making life seem dangerous and unpredictable; but there is a price to pay— "burn out!"

This highly charged state means that the heart is kept under pressure, digestion is weakened and the sexual drive becomes almost non existent. After a time the system can no longer cope and will eventually fail.

THE FIRE ELEMENT AND THE MIND

Fire is often seen as a quality of intelligence, which can be perceived in the alertness and vitality of the eyes. It has a visionary quality to it whereby insights can come into conscious awareness, by-passing the thinking process altogether. It is the stuff of genius. When we have an innovative idea it is commonly depicted as "a light going on"—"Eureka" a new concept is born. This is the creative aspect of fire at work in the mind. It is the process of enlightenment, of "knowing and understanding." Fire is predominately linked to the conscious mind so when we lose consciousness, for whatever reason, then it seems that the light "goes out."

Fire gives the mind direction and purpose. It is closely linked with our will power. All those airy thoughts are all very well but we need fire to grab onto them and start to make them manifest by acting on them. Fire brings great clarity to the mind. A problem with our fire element means that our minds can become muddled and our thinking confused. Fire has the ability to illuminate a subject and throw light onto difficult situations; therefore everything becomes clearer. It can burn through the mists of confusion and delusion like the early morning sun. This clear thinking ability means that there is a decisiveness about fire so that we can cut to the heart of the matter to ensure rapid decision making. The need to create, to do, is a driving force in fire people and as the fire energy is seen as a yang, active energy, it is an energy that many men put to good use in the cut and thrust of big business. But beware, that which can create can often destroy also, and as the fire energy sweeps along it can destroy many ideas, people and places in its path. Too much fire, if it is not coupled with the more compassionate and caring qualities of water, makes for the kind of big business that will surge ahead expanding wildly perhaps at the expense of its workforce or the environment—a case of the ends justifying the means.

If the fire energy is not being expressed freely then the effects are felt in the mind just as surely as they are felt in the body. In this instance, the mind can turn in on itself leading to self-destructive thoughts. The expression of this energy in its natural form is that of positive joy, optimism and a zest for life. Fire, a naturally expansive energy, if it is held in and contained can express itself more negatively as anger, especially as fire types like to create and to have their own way. Of course, as small children learn early on in life, you cannot always have your own way. "No" is often one of the first words we come to understand. If the expression of fire is blocked in this way we become more and more frustrated and angry at the world and the people around us. If we are unable to sustain our energy and get our own way, we can eventually collapse into bitterness and resentment. It is as if the fire runs cold. We become bitter and twisted individuals with a cynical attitude to life.

We saw before how the body responds to the suppression of fire energy by tightening initially in the area of the solar plexus. This suppression of the fire energy in relation to the mind can lead to depression. Our mind becomes dull, nothing seems to matter, vitality drops and lethargy takes over. In this state we can see no way out of our situation. Gone is the razor sharp mind which looks out into the world to embrace life. Instead the thoughts turn inward and we become self-absorbed and eventually the mind can become plagued with obsessive thoughts as the anger and frustration is turned inward. The self-destruct button has been pressed and suicide can be the ultimate escape.

THE FIRE ELEMENT IN COMMUNICATION

Fire people are often very outspoken. Because they can get to the crux of a matter so quickly this direct way of speaking, coupled as it often is with a frightening degree of honesty, can be very upsetting for the recipient and experienced as being very confrontational. With no waffling they get right to the point and can put you embarrassingly on the spot. There is also a precision about their speech and an economy of words; no flowery poetic phrases here. This direct way of communicating is often perceived as aggressive especially if the voice is loud, and can make communicating with them difficult with a natural reaction to clam up under this perceived onslaught.

The fire speech can be very staccato and the words clipped, again leading to abrupt communication. There is often a lot of power and authority in the voice and if it is used negatively, fire people can be bossy, especially as they like their own way a lot of the time. Very often this kind of communication is accompanied by a lot of finger waving and pointing along with the use of the word "you." It is a voice I hear a lot of mothers using with their young children: "You just come here and sit still." "You behave yourself!" It is extremely bossy. Someone who uses fire in this way to communicate most of the time is not listening well. You cannot spend your time ordering people around and also be prepared to listen to their needs and wants. It is almost as if the fiery person is cancelling you out altogether as your thoughts and feelings seem irrelevant. This kind of communication is often done out of the belief that deep down, they have very little self worth and so ordering someone else around and belittling them bolsters them up and feeds their ego. It is the classic bully. In order to have a conversation with someone in this mode you may have to ask him or her to "turn the volume of their speech down a little." It is amazing how much better we hear people when we do not perceive them as shouting at us. However sometimes the fire person can be speaking quite softly but the economy of words and the sharpness of the communication can be perceived as a shout to the listener. Also, you could try asking them if they are interested in what you think or feel about the topic in hand. This can force them to listen and can change the energy of the conversation. Where there is an inability to listen and respond there can be no effective communication. Remember communication is a two way process and we should always be open to the feedback that we receive from another so that we can respond accordingly. Fire people need to learn this lesson.

Fire can also be distinguished in the voice as laughter. I don't mean that a person utilising this particular energy laughs at others but there is a light-hearted, slightly jolly lilt to the voice. Much as we can perceive a twinkle in the eye, this is like a twinkle in the voice. It adds a warmth and friendliness which is appealing and can often soften the directness and candour of fiery speech.

Fire communication can be used to good effect when the speaker uses it to communicate his wishes clearly and succinctly and makes it apparent that he has heard you accurately and is responding to you. For instance if the following question is posed;

"Can you go to the shops for me and pick up some coffee?"

A positive fire response might be:

"Oh, are we out of coffee? I am really busy writing this book at the moment. If you are desperate for a cup now you will have to go to the shops yourself. If you are prepared to wait an hour or so I could go then."

This is a very clear answer. The questioner feels that

the request has been heard but the person responding has also stated his needs, i.e., to continue writing. His needs have been stated also in a very positive way.

A more negative use of fire in communication in answer to that same request might be (in a loud voice, with your nostrils flaring and your face going redder and redder).

"What do you mean we are out of coffee? I'm busy here with this book and you want me to drop everything to run an errand? You drink more coffee than I do so you go. You must have known we were nearly out—can't you even remember to shop properly?"

Which response feels better? Fire used in this negative way means everything that happens is always someone else's fault and you are always on the look out for someone to take the blame—everyone, that is, but you! Communicating constantly in this manner can lead to high blood pressure, headaches and when taken to extreme, can lead to the infliction of actual bodily harm or even, in extreme cases, murder. If you really don't care about the other person and you are always ordering them around and blaming them for all life's problems then you can literally cancel them out by physically attacking them. This is even more likely to happen if both parties are communicating in this element and it is a pattern that occurs a lot in domestic arguments. Watch the flare up that can occur then, with each blaming the other, and hurling insults. A head to head battle is the only outcome. There is no room for compromise or negotiation when you cannot even listen to the other person.

Of all the elements, fire is the one that we are often the most afraid of and rightly so. As small children we are often told off for being loud. Children should be "seen and not heard" as the old Victorian adage goes. Therefore we grow up not knowing how to express fire, as this is the element that we need in order to be loud. Have you ever heard a quiet shout or a silent belly laugh? No, these are naturally vital expressions of this energy. A child that grows up in a family where there is a great deal of shouting between parents or between siblings witnesses the negative effects of such communication (shouting can hurt and wound) and may decide from an early age that they will never shout at another human being. They will never be loud—they will never be angry—they will never be ebullient. In short they will never use fire. This creates difficulties in later life when we need to have this element in our life in order to give clear verbal instructions, infuse our speech with some authority, enthusiasm and, perhaps most importantly, to speak up for ourselves.

Fire energy needs to be expressed freely in any situation where you need to assert yourself, such as when being verbally or physically attacked. This is the nature of the kiai shout, which when used in martial arts is designed to stop others in their tracks and distract them. Fire is utilised when you need to gain attention and a good shout is a way of getting it quickly. It is also necessary when you need to defend your boundaries when someone is overstepping the mark and needs to be made aware of the fact. Using fire energy helps to maintain your boundaries by giving you the ability to say "NO!" and mean it. It is also an energy that enables you to whip up enthusiasm. This element is also essential when you are in a position of leading others and authority and clear-headed thinking are needed.

THE FIRE ELEMENT AND DIET

When man first learnt to harness the element of fire and bring it into his home he started to introduce this element to a lot of the food that he ate. It is important to remember that every time you cook your food you are automatically adding the fire element to it. The sun is another great provider of fire energy to our food. The grains that we grow in the fields, which we leave until they are fully ripened, dried out and turned golden by the sun, encapsulate the energy of fire. Therefore a diet high in bread, cakes, biscuits, pastries and cereals is a diet high in the element of fire. Fire foods are also those that are warming to the body producing internal heat. First class proteins such as meat also fall into this category. Garlic, leeks, onions, ginger, peppers as well as many of the spices are fire foods. All of these foods stimulate the fire element in the blood, increasing circulation and raising body temperature. That is why it is so beneficial to eat these kinds of food during the winter months so that we can conserve our core temperature even when the external environment is freezing. These foods are also beneficial in cases of colds or flu. Hot ginger tea is particularly good when we are "laid low."

The taste associated with this element is bitter. It is interesting to note that all digestive aids are in fact bitter tasting. Even green vegetables, if they are bitter tasting like kale and spinach, are classified under this element.

Adding to the amount of fire energy already in the body encourages the breakdown of foods in the system. A wonderful example of a fire food is coffee. The taste is bitter and we even add extra fire to the beans by roasting them. Coffee is traditionally drunk at the end of a meal and aids in the digestive process. Its very fiery quality enlivens us also and taken at other times during the day without the benefit of a full stomach can lead to the system becoming too fired up and over stimulated. Tea and alcohol are also very stimulating to the system. Eating predominately fiery foods can mean that your digestive system works too fast digesting the food rapidly and leading to poor absorption. Fire type people can take a high proportion of this kind of food and they hardly ever put on weight. They have fast metabolisms and may need to eat little and often during the day to keep going. The bitter taste is one that some people do not like and often they will lessen the taste with the inclusion of sweetness such as taking sugar in strong coffee or adding a little sourness to the taste of spinach or broccoli by adding some lemon juice.

THE FIRE ELEMENT RELATIONSHIPS

We should once again go to nature to understand the interaction of fire with the other elements. Balanced fire has the effect of warming air, which can produce convection currents encouraging air to flow more easily as is its nature. In the body this encourages good circulation. Too much fire and the air is used up. A small room with an open fire becomes very stuffy as the air is used up in the combustion process. So, too, the breakdown of food in our system uses up the air element

59

in order to sustain the fire needed in this process. When there is too little fire it has the effect of chilling the air element within us in us. This makes the circulation sluggish and slows our thinking processes. You may have noticed how it is hard to think straight when you are really cold.

Balanced fire has the effect of warming and encouraging the movement of water. Fire plays an important part in keeping water in its fluid state where it can be of most use to us. Water is a passive element so it needs the effect of the active elements of air and fire to act upon it or it is in danger of stagnating. Excess Fire has the effect of drying out water and taken to extremes leads to desert conditions. In the body this can lead to conditions such as constipation, dry skin and stiffness in the joints as well as inflamed conditions such as ulcerative colitis. In the mind excessive fire can dry up intuition leading to a lack in feeling and compassion. Too little fire and the water turns to ice. Too little fire has the effect of chilling the water so that it becomes difficult for it to flow. Body temperature drops and creativity suffers. Fire and water are the two great creative forces in the universe and by working together in balance much can be achieved. Fire is the original spark of a creative act and can be likened to the determined activity of the sperm. Water can be seen as the receiver of that spark. The ovum with its creative forces works in more sustained long-term way. The balance of the seeming opposites of fire and water is an important one leading to the balance between man's spiritual and earthly nature or, indeed, the balance of the masculine and feminine principles.

Fire has a similar effect on earth as it had on water.

Balanced fire warms the passive earth and enlivens it. In excess, it can dry it out and bake it hard. The earth element in the body has a lot to do with elimination and this would most certainly be affected by too much fire. We would become congested. The mind might also suffer in this way; we can become constipated with old ideas and unable to embrace the new making us rigid and opinionated. Too little fire and the earth is cold and inhospitable and whilst it may be fertile, it is not conducive to growth, much as in the early Springtime when you have to wait for the earth to warm up before seed planting. Ideas which are seeded in the mind need to find the same warmly inviting environment in which to flourish.

GETTING IN TOUCH WITH FIRE

➤ Fire is often the most difficult of all the elements for people to deal with. These exercises are designed so that you can get in touch with the energy of fire and enable you to express it in a controlled way. This way you can come to know the energy of fire and it will lose some of its fear for you. Thus you can utilise more of it in your life instead of being ruled by it. Fire energy is held in the body in the regions of the head, solar plexus and thighs as we have seen; therefore these are important areas to exercise in order to release this element. As stated before, it is easy to get carried away with fire. So it is particularly important that you maintain an awareness of your body whilst performing the following exercises so as not to cause it distress or injury.

➤ Stand with your feet about shoulder width apart.

Keep the body relaxed. Allow the body to drop down into a squat position and at the same time say "Ha" as loudly as possible without straining. You can keep your hands on your thighs throughout this exercise as you pump up and down. Repeat the exercise several times until you become tired. You will notice that your thighs become hot and tired as they are worked in such a dynamic way. Notice, too, the quality of the sound of your "Ha". If it sounds choked or weak your diaphragm and throat are too restricted. Try to relax your abdomen so that the sound can come right up from your belly like a lion's roar and remember to release the jaw. Do not strain during this exercise the body will free up the more you practice. One warning note: do not attempt this exercise if you have knee problems or high blood pressure. Another common response to this is a rush of blood and heat to the head which can make you dizzy. How dynamically you can carry out this exercise will tell you something about how easily you can express your fire. Find a friend to practise with. Get them to stand opposite you and maintain eye contact throughout the procedure. Notice how this feels. If it feels uncomfortable or even threatening or if you are embarrassed then you may not deal with in-coming fire energy well. How do you react when someone shouts at you for instance?

➢ A less strenuous exercise that anyone can do is to stand again with your feet shoulder width apart and raise your arms, palm up, in front of you. Cross the hands over one another, first the left hand over the right, then the right over the left, and the left over the right again. After this move the arms apart until they are both out to the side of your body. As they get to this end point of the movement rise up onto your toes and exclaim "Ha." Bring the arms to the front of the body and repeat. You can also open your eyes wide as you make the sound. This exercise works the legs but in a more gentle way than the previous one and is not heavy on the knees. Moving the arms to the side opens up the chest to allow the sound to be emitted more easily and opening the eyes wide allows the fire energy to show through.

➤ Check out your body temperature. Are you naturally cold or do you suffer from cold hands and feet? If you do, try the exercises above, and try adding some of those warming fire foods and maybe some cayenne pepper to your diet.

➤ Check out how you feel when you are around or involved in a heated argument. If you just want to run and hide, try staying with it for a while. Imagine putting up a screen of fire retardant glass between you and the other person so that you can experience all this fire energy but not get burned by it. Also try asking them if they could turn down the volume a little so that you can hear them better, and they will appear less threatening.

➤ Another sound for getting in touch with the fire element is the sound "OH" as in "snow." The "HA" sound expressed above is a short sound which expels the breath rapidly and as such is a cleansing breath as it removes stale air that gets caught up in the lower regions of the lungs. The "OH" sound should be made with a long slow breath. The mouth makes a perfect circle and the tongue is on the floor of the mouth. Experience the ease, or not, with which the sound is made and feel the vibration in the body. Make the sound for several minutes then stop and stand quietly, experiencing your body. Be aware of the space around you as it continues to silently vibrate with this frequency.

SPIRIT OF WATER

The importance of the Water element has never been lost to man. One of the gods associated with this element was Neptune who for a long while was worshipped on July 23rd to avoid the prospect of drought. He was originally a freshwater god before he was merged with the Greek god, Poseidon, to rule the seas. Man has always built his homes near to a ready supply of this commodity and many early communities were forced to leave their dwellings and move on if the supply of water dried up for some reason. Being able to find water was quite simply a matter of life or death, and still is for many peoples of the earth today, especially those who live in dry, arid conditions. Knowing where to find water was a skill that was much prized, and even today there are those who, with the aid of Hazel twigs, can divine where there is water below the earth. A guide to a rich water source is the presence of trees, which have a great affinity to water, moving thousands of gallons up through their root systems to be released back to the atmosphere through their leaves. They are wonderful circulators of this particular energy. It was thought that trees drew wisdom from the earth up through their roots. So, hugging a tree if you have a problem is not as daft as it may sound!

Water has always been thought to have magical and healing properties. Many churches were built close to wells or springs, and of course there is the purification

65

aspect to water symbolised by baptism. Water was said to have the ability to rid the body of disease and many places that had natural springs became the focus of pilgrimages by the sick who travelled there in the hope of being cured. The most famous of these is Lourdes in France where hundreds of people still travel each year to partake of the holy water. Here in England there is the spring at the Chalice Well in Glastonbury which contains a lot of iron and therefore is said to be especially beneficial for women. The Ganges River in India is said to purify both body and soul, and thousands wash there daily. Of course, there is always an opposite side to things and, as we know, water when polluted or contaminated is also the bringer of disease. Before the days of modern medicine the use of water in controlling fever or reducing swelling was sometimes the only aid to healing that the ancients had.

We are ourselves largely composed of this element which early man was probably not aware of but they did recognise it as the source of all life. We, of course, begin our existence on this planet as aquatic beings in the womb. Even as young babies we retain the ability to exist underwater, a feat that is lost to us as we mature. The very nature of Water is formless. It needs something to contain and channel it and being inert it needs a lot of help from the other elements to enable it to move. It is often thought of as a feminine, passive element, unlike fire whose directness gives it a more masculine feel. In earlier times it was always the women who fetched and carried the water. Water is greatly influenced by the magnetic pull of the moon which causes the changing flow of ocean tides. The moon plays an important part in

66

the menstruation cycles of women as each month, just like the moon itself, the ovum is released, waxes into the time of fruition and then wanes to be released through the menstrual flow each lunar month. Water has long been associated with our emotions and the ability to let them flow and not allow them to dam up where they can wreak havoc. Here is yet another link to the feminine as women generally have easier access to their emotions than men. Water has a link with our depth of feeling which can give rise to strong outbursts of emotions or conversely ineffectiveness and a wishy washy outlook on life. "Still waters run deep" they say and this element has its link to the unconscious mind where can lurk our many demons.

Water has a unique ability. It is a shape changer able to exist in different forms under differing conditions. If the temperature is cold enough it becomes solid and is known as ice and in this guise it has the capability to float and the power to break hard rock. The ancients knew this fact and used it to good effect if they wanted to break or split large rocks. By filling small natural fissures with water they only had to wait for a cold spell of weather and the expansion, that occurred naturally as the water froze, did the hard work for them. Very large boulders could be transported across large distances by another property of water. At 4 degrees centigrade the volume of water in rivers and streams becomes much denser and this coupled with the extra gravitational pull of a full moon means that even large boulders can rise to the surface and are capable of being carried along over some distances. Much of our coastal erosion is caused by water which has collected in cracks and fissures of rock. As the water freezes and expands in winter, it forces the rock apart and sometimes quite large pieces break off. Raise the temperature of water and it reverts back to its fluid state. However if the temperature continues to rise it changes again into a gaseous form and is known as steam or water vapour. Thus, we can see the versatility of this element and its ability to flow and change in response to varying conditions but always with the capability of reverting back to its normal liquid state. Water is also the great universal solvent. A whole host of substances are able to dissolve in water so it enables substances to be transported or absorbed in a more readily accessible state. This is a truly versatile element.

THE WATER ELEMENT IN THE PERSONALITY

"I FEEL—THEREFORE I AM" ✓

Those ruled by this element, which include the water signs of Cancer, Scorpio and Pisces, tend to relate to the world through their emotions and their feeling state. They constantly ask themselves how they feel about another person or new situation so their lives can be ruled by emotionality rather than rational, logical thought. Therefore, their hearts often rule their heads, which can lead to wrong assessments of situations and unclear thinking on occasions. On the other hand, they are usually deeply intuitive and sensitive to both other people and atmospheres. Water is very impressionable. It takes on the form of the vessel in which it is contained so it is easy for a water person to merge with, and if not careful, to lose themselves within another person so that their personality, if not strong, is lost completely. Conversely, they can be very strong, seductive personalities that suck you in and absorb you (remember water is a universal solvent) until you feel lost. If fire is charismatic then water is most definitely magnetic. It exerts an attraction which is subtle and yet never the less powerful.

The feeling natures of water people can make them great carers and healers, able to empathise with others and exhibit great compassion. Their ability to plumb the depths of another human being makes them uncannily intuitive. They seem to be able to tell you what you are feeling before you know it yourself. This ability can make them uncomfortable to be around. The ability to merge with another human being is a challenge for the water type however especially in the healing situation where it is necessary to be clear about what is yours and what is coming from the other person. There is a danger of over identification if they are not careful. However, if you are feeling really emotional about something, it won't phase a water person; but they can have the habit of adding more emotion to the situation so that you feel totally immersed in it, drowning in it even. This watery quality can also make them the classic wet blanket when they become stuck in the more negative emotions and become extremely moody.

The fluidic nature of water enables these people to flow easily from one emotion to another making them appear changeable, volatile and unpredictable to others. Remember that water is a feminine element and so the old wives saying "it being a woman's prerogative to change her mind," has a grain of truth in it. However, she changes her mind at the behest of her changing emotions and take note—she just may have intuited the situation correctly!

THE WATER ELEMENT AND THE BODY

The water type body is usually quite large and well rounded. For a women this means lots of voluptuous curves and a fluid sensuous way of moving. It is no coincidence that the fertility symbols of the world often depict a female form with large breasts and belly as the bearer and supporter of life. The eyes are usually large and soft and have a watery quality to them. The human body is largely composed of water and so it is this element then that rules our basic matrix, as it were. Every single cell in the body is surrounded by and supported in a liquid medium. The water element is vital to the body's growth and maintenance. Every second of our lives cells are dying and being replicated in a continuous cycle of renewal. This continuous process is the prerogative of the water energy in the body along with the help of the earth energy. It can also be said to relate directly to the lymph, the cerebro-spinal fluid, urine, sweat, blood and mucus in the body. It is critical that the correct amount of fluid is maintained in the body. We cannot live long at all without sufficient water and soon become dehydrated. Conversely, too much water in our systems results in fluid retention which creates a different set of problems as the tissues become waterlogged as in oedema; even the lungs can fill up and we can quite literally drown in our own fluids.

The water element governs the transportation system

in the body, being responsible for both carrying nutrients and waste products. It also provides a liquid medium in which the food that we eat is carried through the digestive tract. We are aware of the cleansing effect of this element on the outside of the body but water is crucial to the inner cleansing of the body as well. When we become dehydrated there is a more of a chance of toxins building up in the system and causing problems. There is another important reason why we should keep our bodies well re-hydrated. Energy is water hungry. It is attracted to water and so in order for our whole energy system to function effectively we need sufficient water in the body.

The energy centre for this element is in the pelvis. A part of the body that is closely linked to this energy is our reproductive system. Here is where the creative aspect of water, as distinct from maintenance, comes in. Here is the seat of our greatest creativity in this earthly realm, the ability to form another human life. It is here that the seed pattern or vital force is held. For woman the importance of a well functioning water element is obvious. She needs to be able to get in touch with the receptive quality of this element in order to receive the male sperm, to provide a nurturing and secure liquid environment for her offspring, to sustain a long period of growth and the flexibility to enable her body to expand and change to accommodate the growing size and needs of her child. When her child is born the water element has an important role to play in the production of milk and in the emotional bonding that occurs between mother and infant. As we can see, the water element has a very active role in the whole process of mothering which is not to say that it plays a minor part in the role of the father. His water element has to be well balanced to enable the production of healthy sperm and seminal fluid and to encourage the feelings of caring and compassion for his partner and child. The nurturing energy is just as important in the male as it is in the female even though it may not be so obvious.

The astrological water signs of Cancer, Scorpio and Pisces rule the breasts, genitals and feet respectively. An imbalance in this energy can create problems such as lumps or tenderness in the breasts, thrush, herpes and other problems of the genitals as well as menstrual problems in women and prostate problems in men – maybe even infertility. Sometimes the imbalance will show up in the feet first and quite considerable pain and discomfort is engendered as we walk. As this element has a strong link with the pelvis then not only the pelvis but also the lower back can become affected.

The skin also has an important link to this element as it reacts so readily to our emotions. Spots and rashes can be caused by the water element being out of balance quite often as a result of the fire element seeking expression through angry eruptions and boils. This element has a lot to do with our general sensitivity and an imbalance can cause us to become overly sensitive so that our whole body aches or hurts if it is touched or we may develop allergies which are a sensitivity and an inability to cope with our environment. We lose our watery ability to merge and flow with our surroundings.

THE WATER ELEMENT AND THE MIND

Because the water element has a strong connection to our emotionality it follows that too much water energy can make us too emotional to function properly in a rational way, and too little can mean that our logic and rationality is not tempered by our emotions—we come from our heads and do not listen to our hearts.

Just as physically this element forms the matrix of the body so, too, in the realm of the mind it is the underlying principle or unconscious aspect that maintains the healthy functioning of both body and mind. It is the unconscious mind that is responsible for the second to second survival of the body. We do not have to consciously instruct our heart to keep beating or the oxygen diffusing through the membranes of the lungs, for instance—thank goodness! It leaves the conscious mind free to work on other things. This daily survival responsibility that the unconscious mind has means that it works predominately in patterns. The renewal of cells and organs is the domain of this aspect of mind and it is important that patterns are repeated here or cellular growth can change and get out of hand, as in cancer. In the mind this emphasis on patterns is an important part of our ability to learn. We slot new pieces of information into existing patterns in order to make sense of the world around us. Have you ever driven down a country road at dusk and seen something in the road ahead? Once seen by the eyes our mind scans its memory banks to match that shape to an existing shape or pattern in order to identify it. Firstly we may think it a rabbit, then as we get closer and more of the shape is discernible the mind says it is a bag and finally as we are almost upon it we register that it is in fact a piece of car tyre. So, here we have another very important aspect of this element, memory. Remember water is a passive element. Its ability to receive impressions as well as its properties as a universal solvent means that ideas created in the mind or received by it from external sources sink into it, as it were, and are somehow recorded as on electro-magnetic tape. That water has a memory capability is demonstrated by the practise of homeopathy. Here minute quantities of a substance are dissolved in water and then a tiny proportion of that solution is dissolved in more water and so on and so on until there is nothing discernible left of the original substance. Yet the water somehow has retained the "memory" of it so that it has an active effect. The tissues of the body also retain a cellular memory of events that they have experienced through life. This is why very often when we have a massage or some other form of bodywork, the therapist's hands on a certain part of our anatomy cause us to remember an experience, often but not always traumatic, that has somehow become "trapped" in the body. It is as if the body has recorded everything that has ever happened to us, and when the correct "button" is pressed it re-runs the events.

Because the water element is connected to our memory capability and to our ability to make and match patterns, it can be the cause of the propensity for repeating patterns in our lives. When these patterns are positive and life enhancing then all is well and good; but negative repeating patterns are responsible for recurring illnesses or the desire to always pick the same type of partner and our not so helpful habits like smoking. Because this element is a passive one it can lead to a

74

mind that is easily impressed and therefore easily led. All addictions, including addictive behaviour like not being able to let go of certain relationships, are connected to the water element and we are all addicted to something in our lives to a greater or lesser extent. The water person reacts to the world through feelings and if things are not going well then there is a need to feel better. This is often accomplished through the use of alcohol, drugs, excessive food consumption (especially of the so called comfort foods), and increased dependency on other people. Many eating disorders and co-dependent relationships are a result of an imbalance in this energy. The body has a great propensity for adjusting to the substances that we put in it. The things that we are attracted to, in order to make us feel better, have less of an effect over time, and those uncomfortable feelings that we are trying to ignore can re-surface again. So we need stronger and stronger doses or more and more of our substance of choice to keep us on an even keel. Of course any addiction is detrimental to the mind and body over time. Vitality is lowered, increasing the risk of disease and we become emotionally more and more erratic and undiscriminating.

It is the water element that gives the mind its intuitive sensitivities and the ability to respond to others on an unconscious or psychic level. Having a mind that is too impressionable however can lead to confusion and a loss of a strong sense of self, especially as watery people tend to be "other centred," which is totally consistent with their caring natures. Increased sensitivity means that the boundaries between self and others become blurred. Remember water flows in/around/over/under objects and therefore does not recognise boundaries. Thus it can be hard to distinguish what thoughts and feelings are your own and which truly belong to others.

The water element in relation to the mind gives it a reflective quality in the same way as a still lake acts as a mirror. It adds a certain inward-looking or self-reflective quality to our thinking. This is a very important attribute to possess; if we are constantly acting out our thoughts and feelings in the world without having them balanced by this ability then our capacity for learning is seriously diminished. As soon as we act in the world then we have to be aware of the response that our actions engender and the feedback that we are receiving so that we can then change or modify our actions in relation to that feedback. Then our minds can flow with the ever-changing situations that we find ourselves in, expanding our potential for change and growth enormously.

Like the air element, the water energy can be used in a manipulative way. It is a subtle, yet powerful energy and it can be used to seduce others. There is often a strong sexual component to this energy, which can lead you astray unless you are aware of it. It can be used to hypnotise and exploit the unconscious mind either consciously with intent or often without either party really becoming aware of it, which can lead to some disastrous outcomes. Like the spider in the web, this energy can trap you and draw you in without you recognising what is going on.

As well as ruling our physical ability to procreate, the water element is responsible for all our creative endeavours and keeps our creative juices flowing.

THE WATER ELEMENT IN COMMUNICATION

You can always tell a person who uses a lot of the water element when they talk because it is impossible to have a conversation with them, as you cannot get a word in edgeways. Water flows on and on and on . . . .The words come pouring out like a babbling stream. There is often a fair bit of repetition in their communication as well—remember that propensity for repeating patterns! The use of constant repetition is a classic way of wearing people down and getting your own way. Rather like a tap dripping, this kind of conversation becomes impossible to ignore and we may well find ourselves agreeing just to stop the constant drip that finally erodes away our resolve. This is an element that young children master early on in their lives to get what they want. You can hear them in the sweet shop or toy shop all the time going into whiney watery communication.

"Can I have that ball Mum, hey can I? Richard has a ball just like that, can I have one? Go on Mum let me have it, Pleaseeee Mum, can I have one? Can I? Go on Mum, let me have it. Pleaseeee....."

When the water element is more balanced it leads to lively, flowing conversation and warm mellow tones to the voice. There can be a magnetic or hypnotic quality to it that can suck you in or envelope you and that can prove to be very persuading. Great storytellers utilise this element a lot to keep you on the edge of your seat. The water voice can have a soothing and reassuring effect on the listener and is a good element to utilise with anyone who is very emotionally upset in order to soothe and calm. A lack in this element can lead to an inability to flow a train of thought together in a coherent way and a lack of creative reasoning.

Because the nature of water in the personality is one of compassion and caring it is very easy for someone who uses this element a lot in their communication to end up so concerned about another person that they cancel out themselves, which can leave them feeling powerless and helpless. This can lead to the feeling that without another person they are worthless. The communication can take on a slightly whiny tone as they hold themselves back as they feel unworthy to express an opinion. The resulting constriction in the throat is reflected in the voice. They are constantly trying to please and seeking approval. As is the nature of water they have a tendency to go on and on not always knowing when to stop or when to take no for an answer. A typical watery communication might be:

"Here, can I help you prepare those vegetables? You look so tired. You go and sit down and I'll chop them and put them on to cook. Do you like your carrots sliced lengthways or in small segments? Shall I boil them or steam them? Which do you prefer? Is that all right? Am I doing it the way you like them? Would you like to eat soon or wait until you feel rested? Shall I put them on to cook now ... ...?" and so on.

If the other party in the conversation states that she can prepare the vegetables for herself then the watery response might be:

"No. It's all right. I really don't mind. You sit down and put your feet up. Would you like some tea while you are waiting? Or what about a fruit juice—I know you like

juice. Oh you do look tired, how are you feeling, did you have a bad day today?"

Going too far they can easily draw angry responses from those they try to help, which they take to heart and are extremely upset by. After all they were only trying to help!

If someone communicates all the time in this way they go through life blaming themselves for everything that happens around them and blaming themselves for the other persons' misfortune or unhappiness. The unconscious message is "I don't matter." They become a "yes" person even if inside they disagree with the other person. Do this for long enough and the bitterness that can build up when you constantly eliminate yourself can lead to such disorders as gall stones and cancers.

An example of a more positive water interaction in the circumstances as laid out above might be:

"Hey, you look done in. You have really had a busy day today. I've had nothing much on today so I'd like to use up some energy and cook tea for us both. You put your feet up and I'll tell you when it's ready."

In this way the caring concern for the other person is still there but it comes across in a much more positive and helpful way, as an act that is carried out for the good of both parties and not at the expense of one.

The water mode of communication can be used to best advantage when we need to calm a situation, such as when dealing with a frustrated and angry child. It has a soothing, loving quality to it so it is the tone of voice that we would use in our intimate conversations with those people who we are emotionally close to. It is also the tone of voice that we would employ to seduce or cajole another person.

THE WATER ELEMENT AND DIET

Of course most of the food that we eat has some water content but there are some items that are very watery. These include foods such as melons, squashes, pumpkin, cucumbers and the leafy green vegetables like lettuce. Fish and seaweed that live surrounded by water also fall into this category. The taste associated with the water element is salt and everyone knows if we eat something salty then it makes us want to drink, thus increasing our water intake. Celery is a good example of a water vegetable that has a high salt content.

It is important that we actually drink sufficient water as well to keep our bodies properly hydrated. This is especially important when the climate is hot and dry. In places where the temperature is high but there is little humidity the sweat is evaporated immediately from the skin, which can make living in such a climate more comfortable than one that is hot and humid. But there is a much higher risk of rapid dehydration in dry climates. We have to drink regularly or pretty soon we begin to feel the effects as we lose water from our system. These usually start with headaches and a feeling of disorientation and lead on to nausea and exhaustion. Even in the more temperate climate of the UK most of us do not drink enough. Remember that water is also needed by the body to cleanse and not drinking enough can cause problems with bladder and kidneys. It can lead to constipation, with the stools being too hard and dry to pass easily, which in turn can lead on to haemorrhoid problems. A build up of toxins can also cause headaches and skin problems. Highly emotional, watery people will need to eat plenty of these foods to feed this element which can get overtaxed. It is an interesting fact that someone who is crying a great deal and finds it difficult to stop can help themselves by drinking a couple of pints of water.

THE WATER ELEMENT RELATIONSHIPS

Water will tend to have a dampening effect on all the other elements. Air that is water laden, such as on a humid or foggy day, is hard to breathe. There is not the available oxygen readily available to us and the lungs have to work much harder to extract what we need from the air which tends to make us more tired and heavy feeling. Water laden lungs, where the body produces an over-abundance of mucus as occurs in some asthmatics, is problematic for this same reason. However, the correct amount of water needs to be present in the atmosphere to enable the lungs to function well. Too little and they dry out, and breathing can become rasping and sore.

Water has the very important job of keeping fire in check. In nature an abundance of water ensures that the land does not dry out becoming a desert landscape. Too little water in the human body, and like a car engine with a faulty cooling system, we begin to burn up. As I mentioned in the chapter on fire, fever is a wonderful example of this. Fevers are beneficial to the body because of their cleansing qualities but we don't want to burn the house down! Managing a fever involves the internal and external application of water to keep the fire under control. Cold water compresses on the sacrum are a very effective way of bringing down a temperature.

Too much water in the system can of course put the fire out leading to low body temperature, poor digestion and too much mucus production. It is not a good idea to follow the common practice of drinking water with a meal as this lowers the temperature of the stomach and dilutes the fiery hydrochloric acid of the gastric juices which makes it harder to break down the food. Many of the catarrhal problems that plague us here in Britain can be helped by a break away to somewhere hot and sunny to dry out the sinuses.

Water refreshes the earth. It softens it and makes it more manageable. Too much water and the earth can be washed away, its structure broken down. In the body this occurs in cases of diarrhoea where the faeces has no form and we pass very watery stools. Too little water and the earth can become dry and hard which we experience as constipation. When the earth hardens in this way we lose the fluid movements of the body and the mind and find ourselves rigid and unyielding.

GETTING IN TOUCH WITH WATER.

➤ Get in touch with your emotions by asking yourself what you "feel" about each occurrence in your life. Listen to yourself speaking. If you are asked your opinion and you find yourself answering each time "Well, I *think* we should . . ." then you are answering from your head not your feeling state.

➢ Seek out watery places such lakes, seashores or streams and either physically or emotionally immerse yourself in them.

➢ Work on those areas of the body that are particularly associated with water. Give your feet a regular massage, working out any tension and sore spots that you find. Our feet are generally very neglected parts of our anatomy, so give them a treat and wake up this element at the same time.

➢ Freeing the pelvis is also an important thing to do. The following exercise is a useful one to do (although taking up hula or belly dancing would work just as well). Lie out on the floor with your knees bent and your feet flat on the floor. Imagine that your pelvis has a clock superimposed on it with twelve o'clock just under the navel and six o'clock pointing down towards your groin. Tip your pelvis back and forth so that you move in from twelve o'clock to six o'clock and back again. Do this several times, noticing that when the pelvis is at twelve the lumbar spine flattens onto the floor and when it is at six then the lumbar spine curves. Notice how easy this movement is. Then tilt your pelvis from side to side as if moving from three o'clock across to nine o'clock. Repeat this several times. When these movements feel more fluid begin to circle all around the clock from twelve through three to six then on to nine and back to twelve again. Move in a clockwise direction and then anti-clockwise. Notice how smoothly the pelvis moves and if there is any part of the total movement that feels "clunky" or awkward. Notice how you walk after carrying out this exercise—how does your pelvis feel?

➤ Run yourself a warm bath with 2 cups full of Epsom salts dissolved in it. Make sure you are not disturbed, turn down the lights, maybe put on your favourite soothing music and R e l a x. Feel how the water supports and soothes your body. If you have one nearby, why not try out a floatation tank.

➤ The sound to activate the water element is the sound "OO" as in "Shoe." As before stand in a relaxed manner and practice for a few minutes then stand in silence to experience the effects both internally and externally. Purse the lips, making a small circular shape, place the tongue on the floor of the mouth and proceed as before. Each of the sounds for the elements can be repeated on a daily basis to keep the energy flowing and the body open.

SPIRIT OF EARTH

Earth is perhaps the one element with which people are most familiar. One of the first things that we learn as young children is the ability to trust the earth and to stand and walk upon its surface and master the great unseen force of gravity. How many times were we literally brought down to earth before we learnt this skill! We also learned pretty early on that everything we dropped plummeted to earth and came to rest there. This "attractive" capacity of the gravitational pull is also expressed in the form of magnetism, which is emitted from the planet as another unseen force and which, like gravity, exerts a powerful influence.

The element of earth is the most dense of all the elements. Like the element of water it is seen as a passive feminine force. Linked to fertility it was and still is in many places, revered and worshipped in the form of the earth mother or goddess. It is said that we come from the earth and return to it when we die. The earth is seen as a great provider and its power awakened in many cultures by dance and the stamping of feet or staffs upon the ground. There is a permanency and a stability about earth that is represented in its mountains which are seen as passively powerful and unchanging. However passive it may seem, it is recognised as a potent force, the power of which can be tapped into by man. This has given rise to the practise of the placement of large stones at certain places on the earth's surface where this particular energy can be easily felt or where *ley lines* converge. The stones can either attract or dispel energy in much the same way as acupuncture needles placed along the meridians of the body. It is not definitely known why the ancients erected the great stones of Stonehenge and Avebury as well as the many to be found in the rest of Britain and France, and maybe there was no one reason. However, they obviously thought it very important to do so as many of these stones were hauled over considerable distances with enormous effort to be placed in their final resting place in these sacred areas. Some are certainly to mark burial mounds, memorials to the departed and reminders of our return to earth. Others it is claimed provide a link to the heavens, great terrestrial markers that somehow map the heavens and the passage of the sun through the year. The druids, for instance, worshipped at these stones and they are the sites of many pagan rites and celebrations even in this age.

The ancients worshipped mother earth as the great provider. One of the important items that she provided early man with was shelter and protection. Many early cultures used the natural formation of caves as houses, or utilised the overhang of cliff faces to build beneath to shelter them from rain and snow in the winter and excessive sunshine in summer. There are examples of this use of the natural landscape at Mesa Verde in America where the early Native American Indians built whole cities cleverly tucked under the overhangs of rock. Not only were they protected in this way from the elements but from their enemies. The overhang also provided them with a good source of rainwater as it poured over the cliff top during frequent summer storms.

Spirit of Earth

In Europe man also took to the high ground to build his castles and fortresses. The utilisation of the natural landscape for protection of both home and personnel is also another gift from the earth. Whether man chose to live on the high mountainous places of the earth or deep in its bowels she afforded them protection from natural phenomenon and their sometimes not-so-friendly fellow man.

The resources of the earth have always been used as materials for the actual building of homes. The earth itself, when mixed with water and sometimes straw, can be made into bricks which when baked hard in the sun make excellent building material which is still used in the adobe houses of New Mexico and Spain. Covered with a mud plaster to seal over the bricks gives the houses a rounded, feminine, organic womb-like feel. The thick mud walls keep the houses warm in winter and cool in summer. There is a pleasant feel to living in such dwellings surrounded as you are by this natural basic material. This feeling is not to be found in our modern European architecture made of inorganic materials to precise and uniform dimensions and placed on large lumps of concrete foundations, which cut us off from our contact with the energy of the earth. Some of the older houses in England utilised the same materials as the adobe dwellings despite the very different climate. It is found in the straw and wattle walls of our Tudor houses, for instance. Some of our early farm houses were built of *cob* as it is known. The farmer would take the clay earth and add water to it to make mud. He would then add straw and gravel and allow it to be trampled in by a few of his young bullocks. Each bullock, capable of doing the work of half a dozen men, made the breaking down and mixing that much easier and quicker and any by-products of the bullocks just added to the general cohesiveness of the cob. The mud was not made into bricks, there being a lack of really hot sunshine to bake such things, but piled up layer by layer, allowing time for the mud mixture to harden at each stage before applying more to build up the walls. In some parts of the country there are a few men who still know how to build in this material and are passing the knowledge on.

The earth also freely offers up her stone and rock for the building of houses and with expert construction these dry stone walls are as enduring as any. The other major building material available to early man and also still used today is wood which the earth again provides.

The earth was also worshipped as the provider of that other important commodity for survival, food. Much of this she provided from her own natural store in the form of fruits, berries and edible plant life. Man no doubt learned the hard way which parts of the abundant plant life were good and safe to eat. Pretty soon however, man himself wanted to put down roots and the hunter gatherer lifestyle gave way to settlements and farming of the land to produce crops. What they gained in stability they lost in variety. Mother nature provided far more diverse foods than they were able to grow on their small plots. The nature and condition of the soil, along with the weather conditions, became vital in determining the yield of the crop and so many ceremonies grew up to ensure the fertility of the land and persuade the earth mother to be kind and yield her produce in abundance. In Britain our own corn dollies were made from the last of the summer corn crop to celebrate the yield. They were also powerful symbols of the fertile nature of earth and as such were given to young women to help them conceive. Other more bloody practises were also devised involving animal sacrifice. Blood has always had a strong connection to fertility as people knew from the menstrual cycles of the women. When these cycles stopped they knew that the woman was no longer fertile and could no longer bear fruit. As the provider of new life and our basic needs the earth is also closely linked to that other basic survival instinct, sex.

The earth is seen as solid and dependable and in our modern cultures taken very much for granted and therefore much abused. This particular element has an enormous capacity for absorbing the other elements so it is wonderful to see the level of awareness of many people now increasing leading to the rise of many environmental lobbies who are realising that long suffering as our mother planet is, she cannot keep giving for ever. Likewise, she cannot keep absorbing our waste indefinitely and we should all therefore, learn to be more caring children.

THE EARTH ELEMENT IN THE PERSONALITY

"I HAVE—THEREFORE I AM"

As earth is the most dense of the elements it has much to do with our material world and people with a lot of earth can be very ambitious in their quest for power and prestige because they identify with what they have. The size of their bank balance and their house and car are extremely important to them because they feel it gives a certain status and standing in the community. Their identity and sense of self is linked into what they possess. The astrological sign most identified with this quality is the earth sign of Capricorn and like the mountain goat these people will get to the top by stoic determination and hard work and perseverance. This pre-occupation with the material aspects of life makes them good providers for their families. They also have a helpful and caring nature, which is often expressed in very practical ways. If you take a problem to your earth friend, they will sit quietly and listen and then suggest a host of immediate and practical solutions that you can implement to get out of the hole you find yourself in. They are not necessarily great ideas people but if you want something done, and the stamina to see it through to completion, then an earth person is the one for you. They can possess seemingly endless patience and calm which can be very reassuring.

All the attributes stated above are to be found in the person with a lot of earth in their make-up. Usually solid dependable types, we even call such people "down to earth." No heady flights of fancy for them. Their feet are placed firmly on the ground. Most earthy types are great eaters. They not only really enjoy their food but are also the type who "don't eat to live but live to eat." However, they can be extremely generous with their food and if you visit with them you will surely be well fed and looked after. Their highly sensual natures make them very into their bodies and, along with their love of food, they love to be touched or stroked and hugged. Their earthiness can make them very placid, easy going and slow to anger, but when the earth moves, watch out! Like the planet itself they have an ability to absorb a great deal before they finally erupt. You may be aware of them smouldering below the surface, however, and when they finally let go it is best to get right out of the way.

It is because earth is seen as the element that is most closely aligned with man's basic survival issues, and by this I mean survival of the body, that it is linked so often to what we describe as his animal needs. These include those mentioned above i.e., the need for food, shelter and the procreation of the species. Therefore earth uses and reacts very much through the senses in order to get these needs met and to express the sense of self. If we are "over-earthed" then the pre-occupation with our basic needs and our bodies, coupled with a lot of pragmatism, can stifle the imagination (one of mankind's greatest gifts) dulling the process of enlightenment with doubt.

The slow, practical nature of the earth types and their economy of speech coupled with a certain lack of emotionality, can make the earthy person appear dull and boring. This is especially true of children endowed with a good supply of this element. They often seem to be old for their age and can sometimes find it hard to let go and just have fun. That can be thought of as too frivolous for the hard working earth youngster. The earthiness can give a certain rigidity to their natures which can lead to pickiness which often expresses itself as food fads. The sign of Virgo is known for its obsession to detail, which can appear in both negative nit picking and positive care and pride in their work. The third earth sign of Taurus reflects the earth person's stubborn nature. Taurus is the sign of the bull, so we talk of people being "bull headed" about a subject when they hold strong opinions that are unyielding to argument or persuasion. This immovable quality of earthy types can make them frustrating to be around; but at least you know that they are not going to blow hot and cold, changing their minds every few minutes - on that you can depend!

THE EARTH ELEMENT AND THE BODY

The typical earth body is strong, well built and somewhat square looking. It can be big boned. This is just the kind of body you needed to fulfil a hard day's work geared towards working with the body in a very practical way. Working the land, for instance, which is a very obvious earth activity, requires a body with enough muscle bulk and stamina to dig trenches all day or drive in fence posts until the sun goes down.

The earth body, being so solid, has a downward energy to it. When the person stands or moves there is a sense that their centre of gravity is quite low. This makes them very grounded and therefore hard to push over. It is for this very reason that lowering your centre of gravity to below the navel, which is your *Tan Tien* (as the Chinese call it) or your *Hara* (as it is known in Japan) is so important in martial arts training. This sense of downward energy in some can make the gait appear cumbersome and heavy. Having our centre of gravity down in the pelvis can enable us to be truly centred. By settling down into ourselves as it were, we allow our internal strength to support us and give us a "ground" to move from in our lives. The energy centre for the earth element is located at the coccyx at the base of the spine.

When you look at some people it is easy to see that they are pulling up from the pelvis and their centre of gravity may be somewhere up their chests. This creates tension and rigidity in the body and cuts them off from their sense of inner support and regenerative possibilities as well as their instinctive drives. They will not have what the Buddhists call a Ground of Being and will be cut off from receiving the incoming stream of the Divine Being. Rather as a lightening conductor earths the incoming force of the lightening bolt, so too we need the ability to earth these cosmic forces.

Because the earth element is the most dense of all the elements it stands to reason that it rules the densest of the body's tissues—bone. It is the bones that provide our structure and define our shape and build as well as serving a protective function. The skeleton provides a hard shell for the vital organs of the brain, heart and lungs. The importance of the density of the bones is realised when you hear of children with Brittle Bone disease where the slightest knock causes the bone to shatter. A similar thing can occur in some women as they get older when a drop in their oestrogen level can cause the bones to weaken, as there is a disturbance in the calcium metabolism in the body, and Osteoporosis can develop. The bones help to bear the whole weight of the body and give the muscles something to work against so healthy functioning is vital to this support system. The bones also support in another way by providing blood cells from the bone marrow. If there is a lack of the earth element the bones will weaken as above. If there is too much then arthritis and bone spurs can be the consequences. The idea of support is also mirrored in the astrological sign of Capricorn, which rules the knees. So any problems here can point to an earth disturbance. The knees can become locked back, breaking our connection to the earth and bracing us against life.

The other important functions that this element presides over are those of assimilation (remember the earth has massive capacity for absorption) and the seemingly contrasting function of elimination. It is vital that these two functions are working in harmony to maintain balance. If we continue to absorb and do not eliminate at the same time, the whole system backs up. In the body the small intestine is responsible for a lot of the absorption of nutrients from the food that we eat. This occurs through many tiny finger-like projections called *villi*. These increase the surface area of the intestine and make absorption that much easier. Absorption occurs in other parts of the digestive tract too, for instance, in the colon. Here water is re-absorbed back into the body from the faecal matter as our food passes through our systems in a fluid state. If a large proportion of the water content is not re-absorbed we rapidly dehydrate. This is, of course, what happens when we have diarrhoea. Even the absorption of oxygen into the blood cells can be thought of as a process of earth. In fact any function where a substance is absorbed into the body to help to maintain and build is a product of this element.

Elimination is the ability to let go of substances that are no longer useful and it is essential for healthy maintenance of the body. In this respect the colon is thought of as the major organ of elimination in the body and it is ruled by the astrological sign of Virgo. Many people have problems with their colons, the most

94

common being colitis, spastic colon and haemorrhoids. In order to eliminate freely we need the ability to relax, release and let go. Holding on emotionally and physically, usually because of fear, causes a disturbance in this element. There is also a popular fashion myth in the western world that says that to look good we should have a flat abdomen and many women especially fall prey to this sort of propaganda and tighten their abdominal muscles excessively. Whilst this may give them the ideal model figure, it wrecks havoc with the underlying organs of the pelvis, especially the colon, often making evacuation of the bowels difficult. As we have mentioned before this can lead to an eventual build up of toxins in the body which in turn leads to more problems. Our rigid toilet training also does little to encourage the easy movements of the bowels. Negative programming around the faeces itself means that many people hold on in this area, creating the problems already mentioned as well as gas pains, bloating, general discomfort and pain. If there is a disturbance in the earth element it will effect not only the colon but to some extent all our other elimination processes such as sweating, urinating, breathing and crying. The astrological sign of Taurus rules the neck and any holding here results in a stiff straight neck, leads to difficulties in letting go of our feelings and emotions, and interferes with our ability to communicate. We are usually fearful that if we do let go we will "fall apart," we will not be able to support ourselves or we will be embarrassed or "let our selves down" in some way. These fears lead to excessive holding and rigidity in our bodies and an over use of this element to control. This is made manifest in all the tissues of the body which lose their flexibility and become hard and unyielding. We control out of fear and it is important to recognise and acknowledge this fact, for only then can we change it.

THE EARTH ELEMENT AND THE MIND

Just as the earth element plays a part in our ability to physically root or stabilise our body so, too, it has its reflection in the mind. As a small child many years ago it was common to see a particular toy, which was very popular then, which serves to illustrate the point. It was placed in the cage of pet budgerigars to keep them amused. These toys had a round weighted body and the head was usually that of a bird or a little man. Because of the structure of this toy whenever the caged bird pecked at the head of the toy it would be pushed over but the lead weight in its base always brought it upright again. It may have rolled around and swayed from side to side but it always came back to its centre. If our earth element is balanced then so, too, is our mind, and as life experiences knock us emotionally all over the place, just like the toy, we always have a centre to return to, a place of mental and emotional stability.

Just as this element rules assimilation and elimination in the body, so too it governs those same processes in relation to the mind. It is of vital importance to our everyday functioning and our own personal growth that we have the ability to take on board new information and experiences and be able to assimilate or digest them so as to learn from them. We have all experienced times, I'm sure, when a piece of information just "went in one ear and out the other" or it just did not

96

"sink in." This lack of functioning of the earth element means that there was no ground for it to be seeded in. Therefore there is a tendency for us to repeat experiences and not learn from them because these new ideas have not been assimilated into the psyche. This may be because our minds are so full of old ideas and beliefs that there is no room for any new ones. The old Chinese saying that "you must empty your cup before you can drink of my tea" is particularly apt here.

Our minds can literally become constipated. In the same way as our bodies can become blocked if we do not eliminate then so too our minds. Here is yet another very clear example of how the body and mind are inter-related for a blocked or constipated colon results in fuzzy, unclear thinking.

We need the ability to retain that which serves us well and it is critical that we are also able to let go of that which we no longer need. This principle also holds true for the people in our lives and for the work that we do. How often do we hold on to certain individuals, or a job, that is no longer satisfying, growth promoting, or may be just plain destructive because we are frightened to let go. To give in and let go means to trust and this can be a big issue for those exhibiting an excessive use of this element. There is a real fear of the unknown. The Earth individual's fear of letting go and rapid change leads to excessive control over their own thoughts and action, and also over those people and events around them. The amount of energy tied up in tight, rigid tissues in order to control leaves little energy for much else and vitality can be very low. This can lead to feelings of hopelessness, despondency and despair and perhaps to suicidal thoughts, especially if you feel you are losing the battle to control and life is controlling you. It is very important that we clear the mind regularly. A failure to do so leads to the rigid opinionated thinking and attitudes that can be so characteristic of the earth element. People with a strong earth component to their make-up are often great accumulators and hoarders of facts. Many academics fall into this category. The accumulation of great wealth in material terms that can be so typical of this element is also evident in the wealth of knowledge that certain earth types acquire. If they are not careful, this can lead to a very stuffy, boring and dry individual indeed.

THE EARTH ELEMENT IN COMMUNICATION

As befits the heaviest of all the elements the earth voice tends to be low, slow and deep. The mind works more ponderously than, say, the quick air person, and so communication with an earth person tends to be punctuated with long pauses. This can be so extreme as to leave you wondering if they are going to answer at all sometimes. However, this slow drawl can be very sexy sounding and attractive to some ears. Because an earth person tends to take their time to allow information to sink in and then more time to mull it over before replying, this can lead to frustrating exchanges on occasions. When they do reply the response is usually carefully considered and full of good old fashioned common sense. At times, when we are in a highly emotional state or spinning out of control with a hundred and one things to do, having an earth person around to slow things down, absorb the situation and take control can be very re-assuring. Their calm even temperaments can make their conversation a little mono-syllabic. No great flowery speeches for them, just the facts, pure and simple. The voice, too, is even tempered without much variation in speed or pitch and therefore can lack intonation which can make it sound boring even when the subject matter is not.

In its most positive aspect the earth element, when utilised in communication, is clear and efficient. It gets the message across and, because of earth's emphasis on the practical, gets the job done. A good example of this means of communicating is in the situation where a group of people needs to make a decision on an issue. The air person will be coming up with a myriad of ideas and making his thoughts clear on the subject. The fire person will be suggesting creative ways of getting things moving, while the water person is letting everyone know how they feel about the subject at hand. Having sat and listened to all this and absorbed all the available information the earth type may say something like:

"OK, I hear what you are all saying about this but we do have a limited amount of time available and so I suggest we put aside all this and get down to some concrete ways of getting the job done."

Used in its most negative mode of communication the earth person just regurgitates facts and information interspersed with many references to where the information has come from and who is responsible for it. The classic University lecturer falls into this element. For instance a more negatively earthy talk on the elements might go something like this:

"In the book, entitled Quinta Essentia by Morag

Campbell, she states that the air element has to do with movement. On page 4, we learn that the concept of air energy is known to many cultures. According to the Greeks, for instance, it was known as Pneuma. For further information on the Greek perspective on this we must refer to………"

All the information is there in great precision but it is impersonal, cold and boring. We never get to hear how this person thinks or feels about his subject because he/she is constantly quoting other authorities. There is no emotion present in this presentation and certainly no impassioned speeches. There is nothing of the individual in this communication. In fact, deep down they are probably feeling quite insecure, which is why they rely so heavily on disowning what they are talking about and referencing it to another person. This type of speech is often accompanied by sheets of notes to which they refer constantly. They might as well be a computer! In fact "Star Trek" fans amongst you will recognise this type of person in the character of Data. Because the subject matter is conveyed in such a dry precise way without personal anecdote it can be boring as hell to listen to and pretty soon we switch off!

Earth communication is needed when we want to emphasise or add weight or authority to what we are saying. This is especially important when talking to people in authority like our bank manager or our son's school teacher. We can also use it when we need to slow a conversation down such as the occasions when people are getting carried away and things are getting out of hand. Slowing the conversation down allows time to think before we respond. Slower speech can make us sound more confident and sure of what we are saying, and allows for clarification of a topic. The concept of being well grounded is important to communicate otherwise people will assume that they can verbally push us around and tell us what to do. Adding a little fire to our earth communication will help to establish and keep our boundaries.

THE EARTH ELEMENT AND DIET

The foods that fall into this classification are predominately the root vegetables that grow within the ground. They are heavy, more sustaining and slower to digest than some foods. If we work at a job that demands a great deal of strength and stamina then earth foods are what we need to sustain us over long periods. Some fruit and a hand full of nuts will not suffice! Fats come under this element, which would also include dairy products such as cheese and cream. These foods are harder to digest and therefore tend to slow down the digestive process. If we overdo this kind of food, copious amounts of energy can be diverted from the rest of the body to the digestive tract, in order to break it down. Just think about the traditional Christmas dinner in this country: loads of meat, root vegetables like potatoes and carrots, followed by a very sweet fruit pudding or trifle with lots of cream, then maybe cheese and biscuits and even chocolate to finish. How much energy is available after all that? The taste associated with earth foods is the taste of sweetness. Many of the root vegetables have a natural sweetness to them and, of course, all sugary substances would fall into this category whether in the natural form of honey or in other foods such as sweets and chocolate. We, along with many other creatures it seems, have a real weakness for the taste of sweetness and have to guard against an over indulgence of this particular element. We tend to use the sweet aspect of this element to also fuel the fire element especially with use of highly processed sugary foods which produce a rapid flare-up of energy which soon fizzles out. Too much earthy food, especially if it is not burned up by hard physical work, can lead to a sluggish system and pretty soon a weight gain. Fortunately, we tend to eat more of these types of food in the winter months when we need them to break down slowly and maintain a steady output of heat for the organism. In summer, we naturally turn to more watery foods. Earth foods have a very grounding or "earthing" effect on us and that is also very necessary. If we are feeling spaced out or need building up after a period of illness then these are just the kind of foods that we need. Heavy starches and carbohydrates would also fall under this element.

THE EARTH ELEMENT RELATIONSHIPS

In relation to the other elements earth often has the ability to slow things down. It can ground an air's restless and changeable nature, slowing down their speech and making them less hyperactive. Too much earth however and the air can become immobilised all together. The air and earth energies come together in a dynamic way in the colon where too much earth can slow down the elimination process as earth tend to have a contracting effect. Too little earth and the passage of food through the system can become too rapid.

Balanced earth has the effect of sustaining fire

102

allowing it to burn in a steady controlled way. Too much earth on fire can put the flames out altogether, stifling the creative urge. But just the right amount actually feeds and supports the fire maintaining it in order to see the job through to the end. In the body, too much earth can dampen down the fires of digestion making the system sluggish and unresponsive. If there is not enough earth to support fire in this way then fire tends to be expressed in short blasts of uncoordinated energy sending sparks shooting off in all directions without sustained focus. The fire energy can become unstable, resulting in bursts of vitality followed by periods of lethargy until the earth can build to help support the fire once again.

Earth and water are very compatible elements. The right amount of earth supports and gives form to water, holding it in check like the banks of a river. Too much earth makes the water heavy as in a bog, limiting its ability to flow causing stagnation, which can result in movement difficulties and lymphatic problems for instance. Too little earth, on the other hand, and water rushes everywhere in a deluge of uncontrolled emotionality.

GETTING IN TOUCH WITH EARTH

> As the contact that you are making with the earth is such an important aspect of getting in touch with this element, test for yourself how your feet connect to the earth. Stand in a relaxed posture and become very aware of the soles of your feet and how they make contact to the floor. Ask yourself questions like "How much of my foot is contacting the floor?" and "Through which part of my feet can I feel most of my

body weight falling. Is it the balls of the feet or the heels?" Then find yourself a small, hard rubber ball (a golf ball is ideal for this exercise). Place the ball on the floor in front of you and standing on one foot, place the sole of the other foot on the ball. Begin to slowly move the whole of your foot over the ball so that each part of your foot in turn makes contact with the ball. Do this for up to five minutes. (If you find it difficult to stand on one leg for this length of time you can do the exercise sitting down.) Repeat the same thing on the other foot. Then stand again and become aware of how your feet are connecting with the floor now. Notice the differences then begin to walk slowly around the room and see if there is a more acute feeling of the floor beneath your feet. How is your weight being distributed now? Do you feel that your centre of gravity is lower or that there is a more downward feel to your energy? To further explore grounding, stand with your feet parallel and approximately shoulder width apart. Bend your knees a little and straighten out your lumber spine by tucking your tail under as if about to sit on a high stool. Breathe easily and deeply and imagine that your feet have grown roots that are going deep into the earth. Feel all your body weight falling down through you into the earth. As you continue to breathe easily and deeply, imagine the breath coming in and out through the feet. Really feel that you are solidly attached to the ground. It will help if your weight is a little forward towards the ball of the foot.

➢ Take up gardening. There is something very grounding about squatting or kneeling on the earth and digging in the soil. Watching plants grow encourages that other aspect of the earth personality—patience.

> Visit power spots such as Avebury standing stones in Wiltshire, England where you can make a strong connection to the earth energy.

> Get sensual. Indulge yourself in good meal, massage or a warm aromatic bath. "Enjoy!" Be self indulgent for a change and notice how you feel. If guilt comes up, acknowledge it and go right on enjoying yourself. Tell yourself you deserve it—because you do.

> The sound which activates this energy centre is a long slow "UH" sound. Once again make this sound and allow your body to relax so that it may resonate to this vibration. Keep the pitch of the sound as low as is comfortably possible. Notice where you feel the vibration in your body.

THE ELUSIVE FIFTH ELEMENT
ETHER

And so at last to the Quinta Essentia, the most elusive, most essential, purest and most perfect element which is latent in all things. Because it is not as tangible as the other elements it is often ignored or indeed not known about at all. It is the fundamental space or void out of which the other four elements are made manifest. It cannot be touched or felt, heard or seen and yet it is the underlying matrix of the universe. Because it is not as physical as the other elements it is harder to recognise and to classify. It is subtle and yet powerful. Whilst we are not often aware of its presence, we are certainly aware of its absence as it effect on us is perhaps even more strongly felt than the other elements.

The ether element is neither a positive nor a negative force, neither active nor passive so it is often described as neutral. The word neutral tends to conjure up an image of blandness in most people's mind. A neutral colour is one that blends into the background and is neither one thing nor the other. Another description of ether is that it is the element of balance. Again the image of a static non-dynamic state is conjured up. Nothing could be farther from the truth. The neutral or balanced state that we talk about in relation to this element is in fact a state of great potential. A state, if you like, of dynamic balance. At any moment this potential energy can change into the two

106

opposing forces of the universe, centrifugal or centripetal, masculine or feminine, yang or yin or however you chose to identify them. This potential energy of ether is a powerful state indeed. In the old system of western mysticism the four elements of air, fire, water and earth were seen as the base of a pyramid with the ether element forming the apex. It is the unifying force that unites the other elements and is often likened to spirit. It is an invisible force that pervades all things giving them shape and form and life itself.

It is the underlying vibration of the universe, the initial sound or vibration that created our known universe and holds it together even now. Many peoples of the world still sing ancient chants, which they believe resonate with this vibration and help to ensure that the world remains as we know it. One particular vibration creates each shape and form such as the mountains, rivers or plains, for instance. "Singing" the land ensures its continuity. A particular morning chant helps the sun to rise each day and complete its passage across the skies. The sounds resonate with and evoke the original vibrations of the universe—the universal "Om."

This energy of the ether element can be most easily accessed through meditation, quiet and stillness, because only then can we open ourselves to this energy and feel its presence. It is the Holy Spirit moving through us and it connects us with our source however we perceive it. It is the one constant in our lives, changing and yet unchanging, silent yet speaking volumes, beyond duality. It is difficult for our minds to comprehend, yet we feel its presence in our lives, or as I said before, more often than not we feel its absence more keenly. When we are unable

107

to connect with this energy we have the feeling that there is "something missing" in our lives. We may not be able to quite put our finger on it, but there is a growing realisation that there has to be something more to life than just eating, sleeping and working. Ether is therefore the "essential element" to our sense of connectedness and wellbeing and to the identification of our spiritual nature.

THE ETHER ELEMENT AND THE PERSONALITY

The effects of the various elements on the personality, as was stated before, can be studied in depth within the system of astrology. However, anyone who has studied astrology, even at its most cursory level (which means following the horoscope page in magazines) will know that this system only caters for four elements. This is not to say that the fifth element of ether plays no part in the personality; indeed there are easily identifiable qualities to this element. Someone who is heavily influenced by this element can quite often have a spacey or vacuous quality. They seem not just to float through life but above it with little or nothing seeming to affect them in any strong way. They can be great dreamers but their heads are always up in the clouds and of course they rarely manifest their dreams. Very often they have a feeling of "not belonging"—as if they landed on this planet by some kind of cosmic mistake. These people are very often drawn to a life of meditation or the quite contemplation of the monk or mystic, preferring to live a simple life uninvolved with the rest of mankind. For those who also have a strong connection with the other elements, this element imbues their life with a strong spiritual component and they

108

exhibit real presence.

THE ETHER ELEMENT AND THE BODY

Very often this element leads to an elongation of the body as if reaching up to the heavens and there is an ethereal, slightly frail look to them with a far away look in the eye. Frequently ether people are quite delicately built giving them an air of insubstantiality. The ether element rules all the spaces in the body and there are many more spaces than we realise—we are not as dense as we think! For instance we have a cranial cavity designed not only to house the brain but with sinus spaces that allow for the passage of oxygen and act as resonating chambers so that we can distinguish and make sound. We also have the cavity of the mouth and the digestive tract, the space within the chest that houses the lungs and the spaces in the lungs themselves that allow for the diffusion of gases. Even at the microscopic level it does not matter how small the organism is it still needs space within which to exist. In fact, it is said, that the whole universe is in fact 99% space.

The whole of our body takes up space and needs space in which to move around. Without space there can be no movement and without movement there can be no life. Therefore, the space comes before everything and needs to be present before any of the other elements can manifest. Problems with the ether element in relation to the body can result in breathing difficulties i.e, not enough space in the lungs, or the posture of the chest is too collapsed or restricted to allow for free and easy breathing. All problems with the body in relation to this element are always identifiable as lack of space or constriction and this can affect the body in many ways. A constriction of the upper body or the abdominal cavity for instance leads to problems with the organ functioning in these areas. As ether rules all the spaces in the body it has a strong connection also with the joints as these need to have sufficient space around them to allow for the free and easy movement of the body. When the joints become inflamed or immobilised through the build up of calcium deposits, as in cases of arthritis our movement ability is the first thing to suffer.

As ether is the medium through which the other elements are made manifest and expressed it stands to reason therefore that the ether element has a strong connection with the throat area and it is here that we find the energy centre for this element. It is through the throat that we express our emotions, thoughts and feelings. An energetic blockage of this element will affect the throat leading to an inability to express ourselves, difficulty communicating with others, and physical problems such as tonsillitis and laryngitis.

The ether element has been linked to the sense of hearing and a discord in this particular energy can result in hearing problems such as tinnitus or deafness. The ears are, of course, important organs of balance as well as instruments of hearing. Ether is seen as a very neutral and balanced energy unlike the active, expansive energies of air and fire or the more passive water and earth.

THE ETHER ELEMENT AND THE MIND

The ether element, expressed in the mind, can represent a spacious or even vacuous quality. Many a schoolchild has been asked on occasion "Have you nothing between your ears?" Even as adults there are periods in the day when we often switch off and our minds become blank. However, a state of "no mind" can a very useful state indeed. It gives us a chance to still the frenetic activity of our thought processes and gives space for something new to come in—nature abhorring a vacuum! This state of "no mind" is the state that we can access through meditation or a light trance state which we all slip into periodically throughout the day. I am sure that you have all had the experience of carrying out a repetitive activity, such as making a pot of tea or driving the car, when the mind switches off and we enter into a still and timeless state. When we "come to," the task we were occupied with is completed and we have no recollection of how it was accomplished. Here we have another quality of ether in relation to the mind, and that is its link with time. In this meditative state time takes on a strange, mutable quality, which enables it to seemingly stretch for ever or compress into a moment. On one occasion it may seem that a given task takes forever, and on another occasion, time seems to have flown by and we have completed an activity before we know it. This is when you realise how much of the time our minds are taken up with the concept of "time." It rules and structures our lives. When we slip into this ether space however we turn off the mind, as it were, and are then free from the constraints of time. This freedom enables us to experience another quality of ether and that is its

111

expansiveness. Ether, being space, knows no boundaries. It is open and receptive.

As stated above this element has an important link to the emotions in general and a restriction in ether will result in a constriction of the muscles of the throat and jaw leading to an inability to express any emotions at all. It is not without reason that we describe people who show no emotion or do not express their feelings as "dead from the neck down." The area of the throat is like a chalice or alchemical mixing bowl where the energies of the body flow up and are mixed with the thoughts of the mind and thereby transformed into what we call "emotions." Without this mixing our thoughts are separate from our feelings and the sensations of the body are just that—sensations.

It is here in the throat that the emotion of grief can be most keenly felt as a "lump in the throat" which we often try to choke down. This feeling of grief catches here as we lose connection with people and places such as when they die or we move from place to place leaving the familiar and well loved behind. It is a feeling of being alone and abandoned. It is at these times that many turn outward to religion or inward to reconnect with their own spirituality in order to re-establish a true sense of belonging as we come back to our source which is Love.

The throat needs to be kept open to allow for self expression which is so important to all of us. If we hold back in this area, which can lead to a stiff inflexible holding of the neck, we choke on our words and our self esteem suffers as a result.

We all need to feel that we have a right to be here. A

right to "take up space." A well known insult is to be called "a waste of space." We often talk about our personal space and how we feel when someone invades that space. These space invaders make us feel hemmed in or pinned down, restricted or suffocated. All these feelings make us acutely aware that we do not have enough space, i.e., enough of the ether element in our lives. We often experience this lack of space as a pressure and feel put upon or overloaded, and there is an underlying desire to push everything away, take a deep breath and to feel expanded—to push out the boundaries. When we can expand we can own our own space, our self worth grows, we feel more powerful—even larger than life—and there develops a feeling of well being. This is how we ought to be, open and free with our energies flowing unrestrictedly; able to express ourselves and reach out and embrace life without fear. It is this quality that allows us to feel our connection to the universe, to that undifferentiated energy, to cosmic consciousness, to God, to the Tao, however you perceive it. In our ever growing and increasingly overpopulated world space is becoming a rare commodity. As we are pushed ever more in on ourselves we are in danger of losing our connection to the world around us and are forced to explore instead the vast untapped territory of inner space. A strong connection to the ether element can help us achieve the necessary balance between the two worlds.

THE ETHER ELEMENT AND COMMUNICATION

By now I don't have to tell you how important this element is in our need for self expression. The other

113

elements that we have looked at have a quality associated to the voice whereby we might recognise them. Ether does not have a quality per say, but it affects the voice very directly. We can tell if a person has trouble with this particular element as the field of the throat closes down. If ether is not acknowledged then the throat will be constricted and the voice will sound cracked, broken and strained. The person may frequently need to clear their throat as if they have something stuck in it, which indeed they do. All those unexpressed thoughts and emotions can feel as real as a boulder. It is amazing how large and difficult words seem when we cannot relax the throat and let them just roll out. Sometimes the restriction is so severe that the person can only speak in a very weak voice scarcely above a whisper. This can also be a reflection of the belief that we do not deserve to be here, that we are unimportant i.e., not owning our space, which is our right to exist. With these kinds of feelings we have no right to speak out either. The restriction of the voice can also sometimes be heard with a slightly nasal quality caused by tension in the soft palate of the mouth. It sounds as if we have a permanent head cold. Here the voice is held up in the head and not allowed to descend to the chest and this can be a reflection of an inability to, or fear of, expressing our emotions or our heart felt feelings. We disempower the voice by restricting the air flow from the lungs which normally add power and volume to the voice.

The converse of this, of course, is a throat, mouth and jaw that is relaxed. Provided that the rest of the body, including the diaphragm, is also open the voice has a clear resonant quality to it as it is able to make good use of the natural spaces or resonating chambers that are available to it such as the head, sinuses and chest. It is warm, well rounded and pleasant to listen to and, because it is unrestricted, carries a long way. It is a voice that every stage actor or public speaker needs to perfect. It conveys an aura of self-assurance and confidence and of course it means that the speaker is able to be heard—a very important part of any communication process.

We need to be in touch with ether every time we open our mouth, but especially at times when we need to express ourselves strongly or when we have to address a group and have to project our voice to the back of a large room. We also need to be comfortable with spaces in conversation and not feel that we need to rush to fill the silences. We need to employ this element whenever we want to convey an air of self assurance—in fact all the time!!

THE ETHER ELEMENT AND DIET

The ether element does not have specific foods associated with it as the other elements do. Its subtle aspect resonates more with the aesthetic quality of the dish. If the food is well presented and attractively laid out with a variety of colour, tastes and textures then this element is being well catered for. Food that is of the same or similar colour, or a dish that becomes a habit and is eaten too frequently does not feed this element. Meat, potatoes, peas and carrots as an evening meal every night dulls this element as well as the appetite. It is probably also served in exactly the same way each time with meat in the middle of the plate, peas to the left, carrots and potatoes to the right. Japanese food, which is highly coloured and sculptured to add interest to the dish, is a good example of how the ether element can be introduced in your food. I am not suggesting that we all start to eat raw fish but we can be more adventurous in our cooking and presentation and above all cook with love so that this harmonious feeling is conveyed through the meal to our family or guests. This means taking "time" to prepare food and allowing ourselves sufficient "space" in which to enjoy it. Not too much fast food! Fast food may be all well and good on occasions but neglect the ether quality in our food too much and we will lose the subtle yet so important qualities of this element. Variety and balance in our choice of food leads to improved health and well being.

The general ambience of where we eat plays an important part in this element. Remember ether is contacted most efficiently through those still, quiet times in our life, so let our eating reflect this also. If we are eating then eat. We should not try to read the paper, feed the baby or argue with our spouse at the same time. We should try and make as many mealtimes as possible a time for sharing and connectedness.

THE ETHER ELEMENT RELATIONSHIPS

As already stated ether allows for the manifestation and expression of all the other elements. It sets the stage on which they perform. It could be quite rightly argued that if this particular element is functioning well in our lives then all the others will be as well.

GETTING IN TOUCH WITH ETHER

➤ Try to spend a short time meditating each day. If you have an inability to sit still and meditate then undertake some task that does not require a great deal of mental activity such as gardening or decorating and allow yourself to become fully absorbed in what you are doing. Expand your awareness to take in all the sights and sensations around you but just absorb them and let them seep into you. Do not think about what you are doing or try to analyse yourself. If thoughts do break through, do not be concerned—acknowledge them and continue.

➤ Prepare a colourful and different meal for yourself. Set the table with your best china, adding flowers, candles, your favourite wine and some music. Make the experience as rich as possible and allow yourself lots of time to enjoy it. Examine how it makes you feel and how your body responds to the situation. Be aware of your thoughts—can you just experience the meal without evaluation?

➤ Become aware of the space in your life. When and where do you feel that space is lacking? How do you know when there is not enough space around you? Take notice of the space around you and the home in which you live. How can you create more space; maybe you need to clear the clutter! How do you feel about open spaces or confined spaces? How do you feel when someone invades your space? If you have never thought about it, do so now. Become a space cadet and boldly go!

> The sound to help you get in touch with this element is "AY" as in "hay." The pitch should be comfortably high but do not strain. Once again, take a good deep breath in, and allow the sound to come without straining. The sound should ride on the long, slowly release breath. You will probably experience the sound as resonating in your head.

ELEMENTARY MY DEAR WATSON!

"All Nature, is but Art unknown to thee.

All chance, direction which thou canst not see.

All discord, harmony not understood.

All partial evil, universal good."

Alexander Pope - Essay on Man.

By now I hope that you are coming to recognise the elements more clearly. Some you will know well, others are as strangers. Get to know them all for they are all parts of you. Each one of the elements is related to and dependant upon all of the others. As a community they have to function well and be mutually supportive. "One for all and all for one!" On the great stage of life they each have their parts to play and one poor performance reflects on the whole production. It is easy to recognise when someone is "in their element." They are usually totally absorbed in some activity and having a great deal of enjoyment into the bargain. Working in a garden can be heaven on earth for the earth type. Hot air ballooning is what turns the air type on. Basking in the sun or driving a fast car may be just the thing for the fire type and just try getting a water type to stop soaking in the bath so that the bathroom is free! Whilst being in our own element is great, I hope that you can now see that

119

versatility is the name of the game. The fire person who can never get into water will never be soothing and calm even if the situation calls for that response. The earth type will never inspire and excite staying a stick-in-the-mud all their life. By getting to know the other elements better we can become a more rounded, more colourful, more dynamic human being as we free ourselves from the one dimensional constraints of habitual reaction and explore other ways to express and be.

CYCLE OF THE ELEMENTS

There is a natural cycle to the elements that may have become obvious to you as you have read through this book. First of all there has to be the space for an event to occur. You could also think of this as potential. All around us in the void of the universe there is, held in suspension as it were, a great store of potential energy in a neutral still space. Breaking this stillness, the air element initiates the impulse to move—the thought occurs! That thought has to be acted upon and here comes into play the active element of fire. It provides the will and the determination to carry the thought through to completion. The water element provides the creative force needed to begin to bring that thought to fruition whilst the earth element is the final manifestation of that thought. The planet itself began as a thought in the mind of God and stepped down through all the elements to become manifest. On the seventh day God rested and surveyed all that had been made. This is the reflective still quality of ether and so we are back to where we began ready for another thought to arise out of the space now created by the completion of this first thought. The cycle has completed itself and we are free to proceed again. If we do not allow the cycle to run the full course then we just move back and forth between one or two of the elements tying up our energy and achieving nothing. Imagine if we kept on having brilliant thoughts without the will power to carry them through or we could not sustain that fire and determination so that all our schemes fizzled out to nothing like a damp squib. Maybe we carried an idea through to completion but never sat back and reflected on it. How would we be able to access the worth of the project and learn from it if we did not take the time to step back and take a good look at it?

The need for completion is evident in the physical body as well. We may for example have an instinctual urge to reach out and hug someone but the constraints of society or our own self imposed limitations stop that impulse from being carried out. We freeze the movement and it becomes held in our body as a tension, tying up energy until we can allow the movement to be executed. Once the cycle is allowed to complete then the energy that left that original source can return to it once more and becomes available to us once again for fresh work. Maybe you know someone who fits these profiles or maybe you even recognise yourself here. If the elements do not run full circle and the energy is not allowed to complete, it is held somewhere in the system. Locked away in the body it attracts even more energy to itself and impedes the overall flow of the life force. We become tired and depleted in body and mind. This is how our disease states begin. The element, starved of outward expression, expresses itself internally disrupting our naturally harmonious state. Take a look at the areas in your life where things are left undone; where you have not completed something you started. These areas are holding on to your energy. Recognise them and complete them NOW! Finish that jacket that you were making which is lying at the bottom of your sewing drawer. Complete the project that you promised your boss you would finish three months ago. Make amends to your partner for the hurt that you have caused and do something about finishing that painful relationship that was over months ago and is just dragging on. When you learn to let the energy complete you will find your life transformed. Suddenly there is more energy and vitality available to you. You can become more creative, less stressed and most importantly of all—happier. When you do not have to carry all that unfinished clutter around you will feel a whole lot lighter!

WHEELS WITHIN WHEELS

Even within the natural cycle of the elements there exists another cycle that goes on within the element itself like wheels within wheels. This is the creation and destruction cycle. Each element has its active, or Yang, phase and its passive, more Yin phase. Therefore it follows that each element has the capability to create and to destroy. In the natural world the very air that we breathe can whip up into hurricane force and unleash its destructive power upon us. The sun that warms us and supports growth can burn to a crisp. The same water that sustains and refreshes us can wash us away and drown us. Even good old dependable earth can erupt with terrify destructive force. The elements are beyond morality, beyond duality. It is only our minds that divide their actions into either good or bad depending on the effect that they have on us.

Consider the fire element for instance. In the body this element creates the heat that maintains our core temperature - "That's good!" we say. However, that same fire energy can create fever "That's bad!" The fever drives out the infection destroying invading organisms "That's good!" You see how our minds can work? We constantly judge. If we cannot recognise these natural cycles and go with them then we find ourselves resistant to change because certain things do not fit into our mindscape. Instead, we need to realise that change is the nature of all things and of life itself. Do you want to spend your days struggling and fighting against the natural turn of events or would you rather learn to adapt and adopt new ways of moving to the differing beats of the cosmos?

> **"There is nothing constant in the universe**
> **All ebb and flow,**
> **and every shape that's born,**
> **bears in its womb the seeds of change."**
>
> **Ovid,**
> **Metamorphoses**

A HUMOROUS LOOK AT THE ELEMENTS

We do not have to go back as far as early man to see the influence of the elements on our lives. The early Greeks promoted the concept of the physical world being composed of air, fire, water and earth and Hippocrates, who is often thought of as the founder of modern medicine spoke of the four temperaments. These were a way of classifying people's characteristic make-up. The temperaments resulted in the grouping of people into four basic types that categorised their physical appearance and emotional make-up, body fluids and even the time of year that they were associated with. Good health, they believed, was a question of balancing the basic four fluids of the body, blood, phlegm, black bile and yellow bile.

The elements were known as the four humours. Each humour influenced the temperament of a person and their physiological condition. Their general health and temperament was affected by how the organs associated with a certain fluid functioned. Early physicians would use this type casting when ascertaining what medication to prescribe.

CHOLERIC

The choleric type is associated with the body fluid known as yellow bile and is synonymous with the fire element. Choleric people are hot and dry and they love the summer. They are greatly influenced by the adrenal glands and function a lot from an emotional level. The individual that falls into this category usually has a small head, a large chest and penetrating voice. They tend to walk quickly and are quick to show their anger but also honest, warm hearted and courageous. Their hot temperaments make them very competitive following their chosen pursuit with passion. They are commonly found in the business world. Because of their characteristic need for expression and acceptance they can be liable to hypertension so they need to balance their outward expression with something calming and solitary such as painting, reading or yoga.

MELANCHOLIC

The melancholic is associated with the Autumn and the earth element. They have a tendency to be slow, passive, avaricious and slow to anger. The body fluid they are associated with is black bile, i.e., the secretions of the bile duct and gallbladder, and their temperament is seen as cool an dry. They are sober and serious yet anxious. They are the most introverted of all the humours. Soulful they are often lacking in expression and frequently if not always depressed or pessimistic. This depression can harbour a great deal of hidden aggression which they have trouble expressing. They often have a hard time generating enough energy to get anything done. This lack of energy makes them prone to metabolic problems like poor digestion and thyroid troubles. The melancholic's pessimism means that they resist any kind of change and see little cause for optimism, yet they can be highly responsive to the suffering and needs of others and are often found in the caring professions, religion or the arts. Madness was seen as an imbalance in the four humours and many great minds such as Samuel Johnson and Sir Winston Churchill were plagued with what would be called melancholy. Many of our great poets were in fact of this humour, being given to great introspection, they possessed the ability to reach deep inside and somehow managed to free the energy to express their thoughts and feelings on paper for the benefit of us all. The melancholic, or indeed any of us who find ourselves in this humour during times of great turmoil and crisis, needs to learn how to express and doing anything creative such as writing poetry or acting can help.

PHLEGMATIC

The phlegmatic type reflects the water element and the fluid of phlegm in the body. Winter is their time and cold and moist their temperament. They are usually thin chested individuals with moist skin and large soft eyes. As people they are greatly influenced by the spleen and its secretions that modify the blood and lymph. They, too, are very introverted and can be very heavy to be around. Phlegmatics do not like to become involved with other people and they view themselves as not being easily accepted by others. This can lead to feelings of envy and spite. These people tend towards arthritis and anaemia. They have traditional values and are often pillars of society, stoically carrying out their duties and performing many jobs that others would find boring. If they can overcome their resistance to involvement they make reliable and calm friends. Both the phlegmatic and the melancholic need to understand romantic relationships better which can help to sweeten their bitterness, remove their fear of involvement and raise their excitement levels!

SANGUINE

The fourth element of air is reflected in the sanguine personality. Spring is their allotted time of year and blood the ascribed fluid. The temperament is described as warm and moist. They like nothing better than having fun and enjoying themselves and therefore can be seen by others as being superficial. These beings are physically alert with penetrating minds which became quickly bored so they are often found in jobs that have a variety of activities and maybe a lot of physical movement. They often excel at arts and crafts. They are sociable, easygoing and optimistic. Their constant activity can hide insecurity and they are often great perfectionists. Too much emphasis on perfection and the ensuing stress to achieve it can lead to problems with the colon like diverticulitis and cancer. The need to be perfect can literally eat away at them. The stress caused by this can also lead to heart problems. On the positive side they can overcome this to be great risk-takers and very self-confident individuals. Sanguines need to watch their outlook on life and be less critical of themselves.

Today these classifications have mostly gone out of fashion and we rarely hear them mentioned; but we still talk about people as being "ill-humoured" usually when they are bad tempered and out of sorts, or describe someone as being in "a good humour" when they are fun to be around. It is a shame that more of this ancient way of thinking did not survive into today's medical practises. The early physician put great emphasis on all the aspects of man as an aid to regaining health. It was just as common for him to prescribe listening to music that would benefit his emotions or listening to poetry that would uplift his soul as it was for him to prescribe a potion for his body. Addressing the needs of all the elements was an important part of his health care programme. The practice of natural healing methods and therapies today are much more in tune with this ancient, more holistic way of looking at the individual.

"A tree falls in the forest blocking the path. If a sanguine type came across the tree he would simply jump over it. A choleric person would go home, fetch an axe and return to cut the tree up to clear the path. A phlegmatic type would look to either side to find a way to walk around it. The melancholic on the other hand, when coming across the blocked path, would sit down heavily and cry "Why do these things always happen to me!"

Dedicated to my father Kenneth Rae Williamson,
who first opened my eyes and my heart to the marvels of
the natural world, which has always been, and will ever
continue to be, my unwavering connection to
Divine Spirit.

About the Author

Morag Campbell is a practicing Polarity therapist and Polarity Educator. Based in Devon, England she regularly travels abroad to teach. Having always had a great love and affinity for the natural world she original trained as a Rural Science teacher, where her interests in both science and the natural sciences of Botany and Zoology could be combined to greatest effect. It is therefore little wonder that the elemental aspects of Polarity have always held a fascination for her. Besides teaching and practicing Polarity she runs a regular class in Tai Chi which is another of her loves.

If you would like to contact the author, or are interested in trainings in Polarity Therapy, Morag can be contacted at:

Masterworks International, 27, Old Gloucester Street, London WC1N 3XX Tel: 0780 3173272

Web: http://www.masterworksinternational.com

1987
22

Printed in the United Kingdom
by Lightning Source UK Ltd.
128629UK00001B/356/A